TWO CENTURIES

of

BRITISH WATER-COLOUR PAINTING

Other Works by Adrian Bury

WATER-COLOUR PAINTING OF TODAY
  (*Studio Special Number*)

OIL PAINTING OF TODAY
  (*Studio Special Number*)

THE ART OF REGINALD EVES, R.A.

THOMAS COLLIER, R.I.

JOHN VARLEY OF THE 'OLD SOCIETY'

RICHARD WILSON, THE GRAND CLASSIC

THOMAS ROWLANDSON

TWO CENTURIES

of

BRITISH WATER-COLOUR PAINTING

Compiled by

ADRIAN BURY, HON. R.W.S.

WITH INTRODUCTORY AND
BIOGRAPHICAL NOTES

LONDON

GEORGE NEWNES LIMITED
TOWER HOUSE, SOUTHAMPTON STREET
STRAND, W.C.2

First published in mcml

*Made and Printed in Great Britain
by Purnell and Sons, Limited
Paulton (Somerset) and London*

AUTHOR'S ACKNOWLEDGEMENTS

THE COMPILATION of this anthology of water-colours would have been impossible without a collaborative effort, and I would generally acknowledge the courtesy of artists and collectors who have loaned me originals for the purpose of making colour plates, and of taking such photographs as I needed for monotone reproduction.

The kindly advice of Sir William Russell Flint, P.R.W.S., R.A., and Mr W. L. Lee-Hankey, V.-P.R.W.S., access to the archives of the Royal Society of Painters in Water-Colours, and such information as I have quoted from the *Old Water-Colour Society's Club* volumes, have been a great privilege. Sir Alfred Munnings, P.R.A., and Mr Norman Wilkinson, P.R.I., have taken a friendly interest in this book and helped me in various ways.

Mr Herbert Granville Fell, Editor of *The Connoisseur*, Mr F. Gordon Roe, F.S.A., and Mr Martin Hardie, C.B.E., Hon.R.W.S., have aided me with their scholarly knowledge of the subject. Mr Harry Philp, Secretary of the Royal Society of Painters in Water-Colours, furnished me with particulars about certain drawings and their ownership.

My thanks are due to the many directors, curators and officials of public galleries, in particular to Sir Leigh Ashton of the Victoria and Albert Museum, Mr C. Bernard Stevenson of the Laing Art Gallery, Newcastle-upon-Tyne, and Miss Margaret Pilkington of the Whitworth Art Gallery, Manchester.

I also appreciate the assistance of Mr Augustus Walker of the Walker Galleries, Ltd., New Bond Street, Mr Gerald Agnew of Messrs Thomas Agnew & Sons, Ltd., and Mr E. Proctor Dawbarn of the Fine Art Society, Ltd.

INDEX TO PLATES

IN HALF TONE

IN COLOUR

INTRODUCTION

I T IS the artist's part to love life and show us that it is beautiful, for without him we might well doubt the fact.' So wrote Anatole France. Today's man or woman of fifty, looking back on half a century of experience, will have had cause to wonder about a period of suffering and cruelty unparalleled at any other time, if we take into consideration the vast multitudes involved. The first World War, the squalid, uneasy peace, the second tragedy, the class conflict, with resultant political and social chaos, have left us all somewhat bewildered. Need we assume that such things have always been and always will be? The human conscience has never adopted so cynical an attitude. In the darkest hour the light of hope burns on, and voices of optimism are raised. Old England, once a centre of liberty, poetry and political sagacity, weakened by her mighty efforts to save the world from a long night of tyranny, is recovering. But the Ship of State has been making heavy weather, and the port of security and happiness is still on the horizon. During such times we might well doubt the fact that life is beautiful, but we are none the less reminded of other formidable crises that we have survived by exercising our collective and individual will, with that spiritual aid without which all is in vain.

The late war was won because the British part in it was conducted largely by a man who understood and believed in the unconquerable destiny of our people.

To believe in a nation's greatness is to be aware that the years of frustration are but the prelude to new years of endeavour. It has happened over and over again in our history. As in 1940, so today we must refresh and inspire ourselves with every aspect of Britain's genius.

There is no department of life in which the soul of a nation is so completely revealed as in its art. Here we find idealistic expression—something, at its best, above the tumult of mundane affairs, something attempted and done with no other motive than to show us that life is beautiful and worth living; and if that art is a vital, healthy tradition it is a good augury for the future.

Here in this book I have gathered together a hundred water-colours, representing the whole British School during the past two centuries. They show every facet of a form of expression which is peculiarly, almost exclusively our own. Excepting certain masterpieces of Oriental water-colour painting, Britain is unrivalled in this kind of art; and I believe that a proper understanding of such an achievement gives a key to the national temperament. This mood of idealism, this love of life because it is or can be beautiful, is, I venture to say, part of our spiritual strength.

In his book *Landscape in English Art and Poetry*, Laurence Binyon writes, referring to Blake, 'There is one of his poems which has become almost a second National Anthem. It is everywhere sung by children in our schools.

I will not cease from mental fight,
Nor shall my sword sleep in my hand,
Till we have built Jerusalem
In England's green and pleasant land.

'What did Blake mean by "building Jerusalem"? "Jerusalem" is the ideal city. But Blake does not picture the ideal city as the political and social reformer picture it, with well-built houses, clean streets, good drains, a perfect municipal government. No, it is a city of the mind. Its inhabitants are all to be artists. Perhaps he did not mean that everyone should practise an art. He meant rather that everyone should live in the spirit of the artist, should be a user of imagination, and therefore a dweller in Eternity, the real world. Well, if everyone worked in the spirit of the artist, doing what he had to do as perfectly as he could, finding in that his pleasure, and thinking nothing of gain, would not the world be infinitely better than it is? The world, as it is, is lost in material cares; and therefore instead of rejoicing in the beauty of life men spend their energy in quarrels, jealousies, ambitions, cruelties. What is to redeem the world? It is the power of Imagination. Without imagination each man remains imprisoned in himself. He cannot understand other men. . . .'

All the artists in this book have lived in their imagination, and are therefore dwellers in Eternity. They have gone forth, looked at nature and contemplated the universe, and their gratitude for the life-force has been expressed so memorably and sometimes so perfectly that their drawings are cherished as immortal efforts of genius. Up and down the land we find these works in public and private collections communicating to all who wish it a message of delight.

It is not for me to enter into a history of water-colour painting as it concerns remote ages and peoples. No doubt the troglodytes used the method for their own art. To stain any surface with a tint, of which the vehicle is water, is an obvious enough idea. Colour used with water and yolk of egg was the method of Italian fresco painting, and various great European masters before the eighteenth century occasionally made sketches in water-colours, to aid them in their oil painting. In considering a definite school of water-colour painting, however, it is this country that holds pride of place. For the sake of convenience we may say that the British School began in the eighteenth century with the topographical drawing which recorded views at home or abroad, either of natural or of architectural interest. Some of these drawings were elementary and unambitious. The subject was drawn with a pen outline and tinted conventionally with simple washes of brown, yellow, blue and grey. The artist had no wish to compete with the oil painter, and his attitude was more utilitarian than aesthetic. Frequently these stained drawings were used by engravers, who interpreted them for book and periodical illustration.

A popular subject was the country house. The eighteenth century was an age of fine domestic architecture. In this respect the topographers found many opportunities for their talents. It became the fashion to commission an artist to make a 'portrait' of one's house and parklands; whether the performance was crude or accomplished depended, of course, on the abilities of the performer. Francis Cotes could make a real work of art when he drew, as early as 1750, the water-colour entitled *Landscape with View of a Country Seat* (page 31), now in the Victoria and Albert

Museum. This is much more than a topographical drawing. It is a combination of atmospheric landscape, architecture and figure-drawing, with beautifully realized trees in the foreground, and it proves that the water-colour art was well assured long before its greatest exponents at the end of the eighteenth century were doing their best work.

I mention this drawing by Cotes because it can be too easily assumed that the art developed, as it were, suddenly out of the topographical style. The more one studies it the more convinced one is that all through the century certain men of genius were well aware of the possibilities of the medium as a fine art as distinct from oil painting. Their cumulative influence gradually opened the way for its fullest expression by the younger men.

Paul Sandby, born in 1725, and therefore one of the earliest water-colourists, was both topographical artist and landscape-painter. He worked in transparent tints and in body-colour, and frequently achieved an admirable result. Many of his drawings show that he, too, found the medium adequate for the production of truthful, natural effect. William Pars (1742–82) and John 'Warwick' Smith (1749–1831) were not content with the conventional and artificial stained drawing, but used bright colour and created landscapes rather than mere records of places. Gainsborough had shown with what felicitous charm the landscape could be suggested in rapid impressionistic pencil or chalk sketches washed over with tints. All these artists obviously enjoyed and understood the water-colour medium.

Three forerunners of outstanding genius have yet to be discussed. They are Alexander Cozens, Francis Towne and John Robert Cozens, and may be said to be apart from the limited topographical tradition. They were, in fact, very distinguished as landscape interpreters, and used water-colours with profound imaginative and poetic force.

Francis Nicholson (1753–1844) had discarded the method of achieving a subdued and elementary colour effect. The brilliance and freshness of tint in his work placed him among the inventors of a new style.

Thus the art of landscape drawing and the craft of topography came, hand in hand as it were, down the century. In its last decade they had won considerable public support and were practised by a large number of artists.

Apart from the beauties and antiquities of Britain, inexhaustible as subjects, the grand tour helped in the evolution of the School. Such artists as Pars, Towne and Smith were among the first Englishmen to sketch those classical ruins of Greece, Rome, and the scenes *en route*, that were part of every cultured Englishman's education. The fabulously wealthy Beckford took John Robert Cozens on tour with him, and the Earl of Warwick assisted Smith financially to develop his talent in the Italian environment.

Nor must we forget the eighteenth-century aristocrat as a benefactor to art and artists in general. The hard-drinking, foxhunting squire was not wholly typical of the time of George III. Such personages as the Earl of Essex, the Earl of Dartmouth, the Earl of Hardwicke, Viscount Lascelles, Sir Richard Payne Knight, Sir George Beaumont, Sir Richard Colt Hoare, Lord Farnborough, and Yorkshire landowning families like the Morritts, Cholmeleys and Fawkeses were devoted to art, and some were good amateur artists. It was an age of patronage. These and many other connoisseurs are entitled to credit for encouraging and supporting artists.

Taking a chronological view of the water-colour school as a whole, it is significant how many important artists in this method were born in the third quarter of the eighteenth century. In Edward Dayes, George Barret, Jun., Joshua Cristall, John Glover, Robert Hills, Thomas Girtin and J. M. W. Turner, we have a group who, within twenty-five years, were to expand, enrich and consolidate the tradition, and to hand it on as a perfect vehicle of expression for the hundreds of water-colourists who were to come after them. Dayes (1763–1804) was a powerful draughtsman of buildings and figures, as can be seen from the fine drawing of *The Priory Church, Tynemouth* in the Laing Collection (page 53) and that of *Buckingham House* in the Victoria and Albert Museum. Whatever his temperament, and it appears to have been a tragic one, Dayes was an excellent teacher. He knew that only hard work and discipline could achieve the master-piece—so hard in fact that his pupil of genius, Thomas Girtin (1775–1802), is said to have revolted against what he called the drudgery of copying prints. But Dayes certainly impressed his style on Girtin, and on Turner, as did Thomas Hearne (1744–1817). Both Girtin and Turner are unrivalled as water-colourists. Evolving from the topographical tradition, they accomplished a truly astounding array of magnificent drawings. In their hands the method reaches the fullest expression in dignity and poetic effect.

Four years older than Dayes was Dr Thomas Monro, interesting as an amateur artist but far more important as patron and connoisseur. An enthusiastic collector, with a town house in Adelphi Terrace and country residences at Fetcham and Bushey, Monro was a kind of Maecenas to several young men, including Girtin and Turner, who were to become superb exponents of the art. In an essay published in Volume II of the *Old Water-Colour Society's Club*, the late Dr Foxley Norris, a great-grandson of Monro, gives a lively account of the informal school of water-colour painting which was held at Monro's London house. 'At first,' he writes, 'the young men were set to copy drawings and prints chosen from Thomas Monro's ample collection, and were then taught how to wash in tints of colour. Turner copied drawings by J. R. Cozens and Paul Sandby and Tom Hearne. I have a small and very fine water-colour of a mill by Thomas Hearne (signed)—and my mother has told me that when this was given to her by her father she was told to prize it specially because Mr Turner, then rising to great fame, had had to copy it over and over again as a boy till he got it in every detail to his kindly patron's satisfaction.

'Later on these boys—for some of them were little more—were allowed to do original sketches out of the window, and I have one in sepia of a bridge with barges and the Shot Tower. Whether this is by Turner or Girtin it is difficult to say, but there is very little doubt that it is by one or the other.'

The 'good Dr' introduced his protégés to influential friends and helped to launch them on their careers as artists. This 'academy' lasted some years, for we find John Varley (1778–1842), John Sell Cotman (1782–1842), David Cox (1783–1859), Peter de Wint (1784–1849), A. V. Copley Fielding (1787–1855), and William Henry Hunt (1790–1864) among the young artists at Adelphi Terrace. It is, of course, easy to exaggerate Monro's influence on his pupils. Most of them were boys of genius and would no doubt have fulfilled themselves in any case, but it is an extraordinary fact that he was able to bring together so many water-colourists of excep-tional merit. Cotman, David Cox and de Wint are among the major stars in this group of inspired youth. Cotman's powers of design and skill with the wash, as well as his own aristocratic sense of beauty, place him as high as anybody in the school; de Wint with his exquisite colour sense, audaciously broad brush work, and pastoral mood is also a supreme master; and David Cox, in his many styles, conspicuous for atmospheric effect, yields to none in his handling of rustic scenes, cloud form and general versatility of subject.

The dates are illuminating, and explain why water-colour painting in the first quarter of the nineteenth century had become a department of culture in itself—something incomparably distinguished, encouraged by men of knowledge and taste, and of great interest to the public generally.

As often happens with new movements, the authorities were slow in recognizing its value. The Royal Academy, then occupying rooms at Somerset House, was not sympathetic; and 'since it was only to Somerset House that the water-colour artist who was not content to depend on private patronage only, or on the favour of dealers, could go to exhibit his wares', the art was at a disadvantage as far as display was concerned. With few exceptions water-colours were badly hung 'amidst pictures in oil, but were generally surrounded by such inferior performances as were not deemed worthy of a place in the principal apartment. These were usually subjects ill-conceived, badly drawn and worse coloured—garish and staring in effect—and commonly so entirely at variance with harmony as not only to excite disgust in the spectator, but by the violence of their opposition, to do manifest injury to the chaste and unobtrusive works in water-colours.'[1] The writer of the foregoing, William Henry Pyne, one of the foundation members of the Society of Painters in Water-Colours, wrote with some feeling of rancour. The water-colourists, however, do appear to have had a grievance, and determined to found a society of their own, particularly since no artist who worked exclusively in this method could compete for academic honours, thanks to a rule in the original foundation of the Royal Academy—a rule that was changed only in 1942.

As early as the first or second year of the nineteenth century, W. F. Wells, friend of the great Turner, endeavoured to form such an association, but fear of offending members of the Royal Academy delayed the project until 1804, when ten artists met on November 30 at the Stratford Coffee House in Oxford Street, drew up a set of rules, and formally assumed the title of the Society of Painters in Water-Colours. Six other artists were invited to join. An exhibition was arranged at 20 Lower Brook Street, and was opened on April 22, 1805. It was an overwhelming success. Nearly 12,000 people paid for admission, many pictures were sold, and the art of water-colour painting became definitely established and universally approved by the connoisseurs, Press and public.

Certain facts, not generally realized, went to the making of that success. However dubious the members were about having an exhibition to themselves, they could have had no doubt as to the quality of the work to be shown. Although Girtin, who had died in 1802, Turner, Cotman, de Wint and Cox were not among the original members, all the artists who were had great ability and some had outstanding gifts. They had not been experimenting with new theories and eccentric techniques. They were all masters of their craft. Though a few of them were very young men, the average age of the sixteen was thirty-eight.

[1] W. H. Pyne, *Somerset House Gazette*, p. 130.

I need not detail the vicissitudes of this society, its phenomenal success in the first decade of the nineteenth century, its difficulties, its changes of policy after 1812 and reversion to its original objective in 1820. After nearly one hundred and fifty years this society is still a potent influence in art, attracts the best talent, and holds pride of place among all the societies devoted to water-colour painting.

After 1805 other groups came into being as a result of the general enthusiasm: the Associated Artists in Water-Colours, which lasted from 1808 till 1813, and in 1832 the New Society, which still happily exists as the Royal Institute of Painters in Water-Colours.

Reverting to the School as a whole, the year 1805 may be taken as a focal point in the story. The formal recognition of the art as distinct in itself increased the interest and number of amateurs and persons wishing to learn. Many of the earlier masters—Alexander Cozens, Paul Sandby, Edward Dayes, and John Glover, for instance—had a number of pupils, but the exhibition in Brook Street so stimulated the public that water-colourists were besieged with requests to teach. Some manuscript notes for a biographical notice of Francis Nicholson, a foundation member of the Society of Painters in Water-Colours, inform us that the 'opening of the Water Color [sic] Exhibition in the year 1805 may be dated as the commencement of Mr Nicholson's fame and success in London. In conjunction with Glover, Varley, Prout and others, an advance in the art of Water-Colour painting was made such as to astonish and call forth the admiration of the Public. The next step, after admiring, was to imitate the works of these Artists, and for some years after their doors were beset and the streets where they resided thronged with the Carriages of the nobility and gentry. They eagerly paid their guinea an hour for the privilege of witnessing the progress of a picture by the favourite Professor. To such a degree was this mania carried that every hour of the day was devoted to this easy and lucrative employment, and the more difficulty there was found in obtaining admission, the greater of course became the anxiety to gain it.'[1]

Girtin, Cotman, Cox and de Wint also spent a considerable part of their lives as drawing-masters. Not infrequently, amateurs carried their work far beyond what was termed a polite accomplishment, and the number of old but anonymous water-colours that reach the sale-rooms is proof of the skill of unprofessional performers. To John Varley, most popular of all drawing masters, it happened that many of his pupils became famous artists and left works that are prized and collected. This desire to learn the art sharpened the critical faculties of the public, and stimulated, in turn, the efforts of the masters themselves. Art is at its best in a society where artist and patron understand one another, and perhaps at no time in England before or since the opening years of the nineteenth century has this mutual agreement been so strong and so fruitful of good work.

From about 1790 to 1830, to be able to draw and to tint was regarded as a necessary part of education, just as in Elizabethan times hardly anybody could claim to be cultured unless he had attempted to write a sonnet or a lyric.

Laurence Binyon has skilfully developed the theme of the alliance between landscape art and poetry. It is a valuable theory and, I believe, fundamental to our school of water-colour painting. Here, maybe, is the explanation of the art's origin. That lyrical sense of beauty, that

[1] *Old Water-Colour Society's Club, Volume VIII* (1930-1).

love of the landscape which has found perfect expression in English poetry was extended to English art as soon as artists had obtained a method applicable to their emotions. The water-colour art was a technical novelty and expedient rather than a new spiritual experience, and to say that it began in the eighteenth century is to deprive it of far older instincts and associations. We have only to read Milton's *L'Allegro* to see how strong is the link between the poets and the painters. Our water-colour school of landscape is enshrined in the following lines:

Streit mine eye hath caught new pleasures
Whilst the Lantskip round it measures,
Russet Lawns and Fallows gray,
Where the nibbling flocks do stray,
Mountains on whose barren brest
The labouring clouds do often rest:
Meadows trim with Daisies pide,
Shallow Brooks and Rivers wide.
Towers, and Battlements it sees,
Boosom'd high in tufted Trees.

An artist of imagination, such as Samuel Palmer, could paint several pictures from these ten lines. Over and over again we notice how they apply to various drawings. Just as the 'lantskip' moved Milton and other poets to song, so did it move water-colourists to express themselves in their chosen medium. The inspiration is the same, and in the best water-colours the method is not dissimilar—quick observation, sentiment and thought, clarity of touch, and as little revision as possible. With the masters of either art the 'song' is sung with all the ardour of which they are capable, and is warm, glowing and impulsive.

The poetic word anticipates the drawing, all through the sixteenth, seventeenth and eighteenth centuries. The Elizabethans are full of allusions to the landscape, and earlier and later poets have revelled in that love of nature which is, of course, the basis of landscape painting. I suggest that the water-colour art is just another form of the English genius for lyrical poetry, a genius that produced the illuminated manuscript, the decorative details of our cathedrals, and such early poems as 'The Happy Land' from *The Phoenix*; 'The Riddle of the Sun and Moon'; and 'Sumer is icumen in', and 'Springtide', written at the beginning of the thirteenth century. When we look at the thirteenth-century roundel of the Madonna and Child in the Bishop of Chichester's palace, or the stained-glass Jesse window at York, we are aware that our forefathers possessed a gift of happiness and inspiration that tended to make beauty out of life and its mysteries. This mood was linked with a strong faith in the invisible and eternal. The love of nature and of religion, the desire for joy in this world and hope of it in the next, resulted in a just balance of the practical and mystical—a *trait* of great consequence in the evolution of our people, a virtue, indeed, that supported us throughout all the vicissitudes of history, and continues to this day in spite of politico-scientific materialism. Our water-colourists are the inheritors and exponents of a sense of beauty and mystery of things deeply rooted in the English temperament.

This sense is common, no doubt, to all cultured peoples, but why other nations have not been able to express themselves so splendidly in water-colour is because their climates are unsuitable to the art. Though we complain about our weather we have only to live in the tropics or Mediterranean lands to realize that it is by no means inclement. With neither extremes of heat nor cold, the landscape has beauty at all times of the year. Its moist atmosphere is responsible for great wealth of colour and cloud-form. Its variability, its discreet dawns and slow-moving sunsets are the essence of the art. Its mysteriously blue distances and tremulous atmosphere are irresistibly evocative. There is endless variety in the landscape—plain and mountain, woodland, river and lake, and all so easily accessible, with the sea at every point of the compass. Centuries of civilization have enriched our island with superb architecture. Picturesque ruins abound everywhere. To know our own country well is to be aware of an infinite treasury of natural beauty. When our artists had become aware of it, when they had found a quick method to express it, the water-colour art was a foregone conclusion. And it so happened that, coinciding with the rise of the School, men were able to travel about with some speed and safety for the first time since the Romans had been in occupation. The very efficient coaching system had made this possible. In trying to assess the magic and mastery of the art during the fifty years between 1780 and 1830 we must remember that places like Wales and the Lake District, Devonshire, Suffolk, Yorkshire—all the 'coloured countries'—had only just been discovered by metropolitan artists and public.

How the artists responded to those 'realms of gold'! They took the coach or they rode on horseback. Turner is exploring Wales on a pony; Girtin is off to Harewood to stay with 'Prince' Lascelles and paint Yorkshire scenes; Cotman, the Varleys and de Wint are moving about from beauty spot to beauty spot. Most of the early masters appear to have travelled the whole of England and Wales. Some went also to Scotland and Ireland. One can imagine with what enthusiasm the foundation members of the 'Old Society' exchanged experiences and showed one another their water-colours painted on tour. Frequently they sketched the same famous subject. The opening years of the nineteenth century, particularly, must have been an inspiring period for landscape-painters, a time when the poetry of nature 'harmonized' the moods and the desires of men and women of vision and refinement.

Apart from the drawings themselves, the 'Old Society' catalogues are full of quotations from the poets, as if the artists had happily confirmed the lines of their favourite authors, for it was then the custom to accompany exhibits with long excerpts from the classics. Some of these artists were poets as well, such as George Barret, Jun., Francis Oliver Finch and Samuel Palmer.

The exhibitions at the 'Old Society' were great events in London's artistic and social life. It would appear that about water-colour landscape there was no mystification and little conflict of opinion. It was a language that everybody understood. The artists put down what they saw and what the public could see. There were no 'isms'. It remained to a later age to stultify the meaning of art with sterile theories. Beauty, a century or more ago, meant something to the world. The very word had not become a term which drew forth contempt from the sophisticated mind. There was no affectation. Fine drawing following natural form and colour was enough. It was, moreover, a moment of hope and courage, notwithstanding the fact that the first exhibition of the 'Old Society' took place in the middle of the Napoleonic wars.

Those wars had closed the Continent to English artists, except for a brief interval (1802–3) after the peace of Amiens, when a few water-colourists made a hurried visit to France. One was Girtin, who did some of his finest drawings in Paris. The defeat of Napoleon at Waterloo, however, opened the Continent again, and the artists sought new subjects in France, Italy, Germany and the Middle East. Men born at the beginning of the nineteenth century, R. P. Bonington, William Callow, T. S. Boys, W. J. Mueller, James Holland and many others, are taking the grand tour anew and bringing back hundreds of sketches which will reveal to the public the medieval beauties of Continental cities. The drawings of the eighteen-twenties are consistently richer in colour, and this may be due partly to the sunnier southern climates and partly to the fact that there was a general increase in the use of colour. The brilliant works in oils by Turner, Constable and William Havell must have had their influence on water-colourists—sometimes for the worse—since we find not a few of them, notably John Varley, trying to compete with the oil painters in this respect. As time went on this competition became more pronounced, modifying the water-colour technique and making for detail and high finish.

The effort to supply an ever-increasing demand for pictures of some kind or another tended to put quantity before quality. The prodigious number of exhibits by certain popular artists at the 'Old Society' (Copley Fielding showed no fewer than 1748 during his career) prove virtuosity rather than inspiration. The Victorian era was a time of great prosperity for water-colourists. The public enjoyed both the originals and the engravings that were made from them for such Annuals as the *Forget-Me-Not, Keepsake* and *Souvenir.* These publications kept the popular artists busy. Before long the steel engraving was abandoned for the chromo-lithograph, the coloured woodcut, and finally, as in our own time, the process-colour plate.

These methods for circulating art far and wide had a marked influence on water-colour painting itself. The golden age, when it was sufficient to paint a masterpiece of atmospheric effect, suffered a decline due to a decline in taste. The aristocratic patron had passed or was passing, and the bourgeoisie were the arbiters. Aesthetic values were confused. This is not to say that much conscientious work was not done during the second half of the nineteenth century, but it depended upon technique rather than idealistic expression. As the old masters died off one by one we find fewer artists of real genius in water-colour to take their place. It never happened again that so many supreme water-colourists were born approximately at the same time. Here and there the master arrives, Thomas Collier (1840–91), for instance, who returned to the original source of inspiration, nature, and to the forerunners of the school; and in each decade from the 'fifties to the end of the century somebody of consequence was born who ultimately used the medium with great power and originality. We recall the names of George Clausen, Frank Brangwyn, John Sargent, Arthur Melville, Wilson Steer and Joseph Crawhall. (With the exception of Crawhall and Melville these artists were also great oil painters.) But they are all conspicuous in a period that shows signs of revival in the first decade of the twentieth century. What also contributed to that revival was the interest in and enthusiasm for the founders of the School. This was brought about largely by scholarly research into the history of our water-colour painters, and by admirable colour reproductions that appeared in books and art magazines. Better knowledge of the old masters, insistence on fine drawing, and the belief that a good water-colour can be a work of art in itself and need not necessarily be done as an illustration with historical, sentimental or anecdotal significance, helped. Subjects are now chosen with greater discrimination. The fashion for tight work and stipple has given place to the direct, lucid application of tints. The artist is free again to express his poetic reactions towards form and colour and atmosphere, and the result is not only a higher standard of technique but greater variety of subjects. The lyrical note has returned, and is to be seen at all the exhibitions where water-colours are shown.

As to the plates in this book, the reader will notice that I have not included any works, even by artists of some celebrity, that do not conform to the normal intelligent vision and expert handling of the medium. Hence, drawings with a cubistic, surrealistic, or childlike affectation are omitted because I am of the opinion that they are aesthetic aberrations and will not, however ingenious and sophisticated the argument, fit into the great tradition. Nor have I included, with two exceptions, records of the late war. While I admire some of the drawings done so devotedly on various fronts and at home, the general tendency of such work was necessarily hurried and journalistic. Actual war and its effects, except for bomb damage which offered artists a tragic wealth of neo-ruins, is hardly a theme for the exercise of so subtle and exacting a medium as water-colour.

Certain examples reproduced in this book are among the great classics. If the connoisseur fails to find his own special gem I can only excuse myself by saying that the number of plates had perforce to be limited. Sometimes I have purposely avoided a water-colour too well known that I might offer a lesser known example. If certain fine contemporary water-colourists are not represented, no reflection on their merits is intended. Again, I must plead lack of space.

The variety of styles and subjects is enough to prove that, given personality in the artist, the tradition is capable of illimitable improvisation without resort to eccentricity. Pictures must speak for themselves, but some reference to outstanding masterpieces, groups of men who influenced one another, and their relationship to the School as a whole, is pertinent to the theme.

A supreme effort of the imagination is John Robert Cozens' *View in the Island of Elba* (page 41). Here in a space no larger than $14\frac{1}{2}$ by $21\frac{1}{8}$ inches is a sombre vision of a vast rocky solitude that haunts the mind. To have reduced these mighty stones to so brief a synthesis, and still to have retained the essential facts of nature with the formidable spirit of the scene is the work of a great mind. It is possible that Cozens experienced the same mood as did Richard Wilson looking at Snowdon and the summit of Cader Idris; but, whether influenced or not by the 'Father of English Landscape', here is a magnificent drawing, and one quite indispensable to the theme of mountains which was to become an ever-inspiring subject for water-colourists. Though Constable exaggerated when he said that Cozens was the greatest artist who ever touched landscape, Cozens is certainly unique as an interpreter of the mountain mood. The drawing was done when the artist was twenty-eight and at the height of his powers. The younger men, Girtin and Turner especially, may well have responded to such a work and felt a clarification of their own aspiring vision. They were great enough in youth to enter into the sublime solitude of this masterpiece, and it may have helped them on the way to such works as Girtin's *Fells near Bolton, Yorkshire* and those mountain pieces to be found in Turner's *Hereford Court Sketch-Book* now in the British Museum; but the influence was one of vision rather than technique, for Cozens, as a technician, has none of the certainty of Girtin and Turner.

Another magnificent mountain drawing is John Sell Cotman's *Cader Idris from Barmouth Sands* (page 87), formerly in Mr F. J. Nettlefold's collection and presented by him to the Diploma Gallery of the Royal Society of Painters in Water-Colours. It is one of this artist's finest drawings, dates probably from his early twenties, and is under Girtin's influence. It has such grandeur of vision, perfect arrangement of light and dark shapes, warm and cool colour, as to take its place among the masterpieces.

After these solemn views of nature we can, by way of contrast, contemplate David Wilkie's *Village Festival* (page 93), with its loquacious, gregarious human society—an occasion of laughter, song and dance—so typical of this master's love and observation of popular gatherings. This is rare water-colour, in the sense that I have seen no others by Wilkie approximating to its completeness. It proves how accomplished this artist could be in the water-colour medium. It was discovered by Mr Alfred Egerton Cooper, and has impressed and surprised all who have seen it as a brilliant work by the painter of the famous *The Penny Wedding* and *Chelsea Pensioners Listening to the News of Waterloo*.

I have always regarded Peter de Wint's *Valley of the Thames and Cliveden Woods* as an outstanding specimen of this master's landscapes. The clarification of this vast and luxuriant scene demands not only impeccable craftsmanship but intense feeling. The selective power shown in this water-colour is the result of a profound analysis of nature in mass and in detail. De Wint has entered into the *genius loci* with astounding intuition. The whole apparatus of a summer day in one of the most beautiful parts of England has been reverently taken to pieces, as it were, and reconstructed for the purposes of art. In the massing of the woodlands, the simplification of the foreground, and general atmospheric recession, it is a great effort, fresh and inspired from the first to the last stroke of the brush.

De Wint had the power of suggesting details. John Frederick Lewis left nothing to the imagination. Discussing his work in *The Art Journal* for February 1858, a critic remarks that this artist's picture, *Life in the Harem*, was 'the most extraordinary production ever executed in water-colours'. The remark might well apply to the version of the same subject reproduced in this book (page 163). Lewis is unique for a combination of breadth and high finish. There is a finality about his style that places him with the Dutch interior painters in oil. Even so, he out-details them, revelling in minute ornament, architectural or sartorial, and smoothness of surface. He sought to do with water-colours what had been thought possible only with oils. *Life in the Harem* is indeed a marvel of skill, but I am yet to be convinced that it is a supreme effort of the mind. The drawing is too accurate, too consciously wrought to come into the category of inspiration.

Genius, of course, is a timeless quality, and when or how it will express itself is incalculable. Of the many drawings in this book, Samuel Palmer's *Hailsham—Sussex. Storm Coming On* (page 115) is a startling manifestation of premature knowledge. This water-colour was done in 1821 when Palmer was only sixteen, and I cannot recall a work by any other water-colourist of the same age that so completely foreshadows the great career to come. The fact that it is not typical of Palmer's work is all the more interesting; but it does show how powerfully nature affected him as a boy, and with what nervous strength he could identify himself with the drama of the elements. Critics when confronted with so original an impression are apt to say 'How modern!' It is a misleading term. In great landscape painting there is no such thing as a modern or ancient style. The only difference today is that we do accept and appreciate the sketch as a work of art in itself—perhaps a little too readily sometimes, but in the case of this drawing by Palmer we have no need to be diffident. It is a truly wonderful work. This artist's water-colours, as a whole, have a mysterious charm, as if nature had undergone some magical transformation for the purposes of art. It is curious that as late as 1846, when the artist had turned forty, he was preoccupied with what he called a 'New Style' and 'Bold Effect'.

Let us consider Richard Parkes Bonington's *Sunset in the Pays de Caux* (page 95). At first a satellite of Constable, he became a major star in his own right within the period of his all too brief career. He died at the age of twenty-six in 1828. Bonington was, moreover, a kind of ambassador of culture between the English and French schools, further intensifying the 'light' which had been taken to France with Constable's picture *The Haywain* in 1823. Working for some years in France, Bonington was much admired by French artists. Delacroix, his great friend, has written that 'No one in the modern school, perhaps no earlier artist, possessed the ease of execution which makes his works, in a certain sense, diamonds, by which the eye is pleased and fascinated, quite independently of the subject and the particular representation of nature'. It is the truthful effect of light that Delacroix had in mind when he wrote these words; and it will be recalled how impressed he was by the same quality in Constable's pictures. The *Sunset in the Pays de Caux* is not only a triumph of skill. In sentiment it is one of the most enchanting water-colours ever painted. Here is a perfect summer evening on the French coast, a fleeting hour of beauty crystallized and held fast against time as by some divine ingenuity.

A remarkably exciting drawing is *The Haywain* in the collection of Mr Leonard Duke. It puzzled me and other experts when we first saw it—obviously a sketch of Constable's *The Haywain* in the Victoria and Albert Museum. The question arose as to who could have done this powerful impression, since the drawing has all the courage of Constable's genius. It was certainly by somebody who, for a brief moment, was absolutely *en rapport* with Constable himself. Interpretation, none the less, from an oil masterpiece, it could have been done only by a brilliant sketcher and supreme colourist. Was it an improvisation on Constable by Sargent or Wilson Steer, either of whom might have become so enamoured of the original as to translate it so effectively into water-colours? A more likely artist, however, is credited with this attractive work—Hercules Brabazon Brabazon.[1] Some other drawings in the same vein by this artist came on the market in 1946, and we can assume that *The Haywain* water-colour was done by this Squire of Seddlescombe, whose extraordinary gifts and life are briefly described on page 164.

Thomas Collier, born in 1840, is certainly among the masters, and it is singular that, at a time when breadth of style and brilliant atmospheric effect had gone out of fashion, Collier persisted in the grand manner of water-colour painting. Influenced by David Cox and Constable, he strove for absolute truth to nature, evolving a style that simplifies while it illuminates the most complex themes. Collier was described by Sir James Linton, P.R.I., as the 'last of the great sketchers'. There is a grandeur about his moorland scenes that surpasses the work of all other water-colourists who attempted this subject. Collier, in certain works, is regarded as the finest of sky-painters, his handling of large, rapidly moving clouds being little short of miraculous. The unifying touch in his work is the result of a comprehensive vision of the whole scene from the immediate foreground to the zenith. In his youth he devoted himself to Welsh subjects in the neighbourhood of Bettws-y-Coed. He came south in the eighteen-

---

[1] With the owner's agreement I have taken this line. The fact remains that more than one expert believes this water-colour to be by Constable himself.

seventies and painted much in the neighbourhood of Arundel; one of his pictures, *Arundel Castle from the Park* (1875), won him the Legion of Honour when exhibited in Paris. *Stacking Peat, Festiniog, North Wales* (page 123), was presented by Mr F. J. Nettlefold to the National Library of Wales in 1948.

Animal painters in water-colour are not numerous. The most distinguished of them was Joseph Crawhall. The drawing *Greyhound* (page 139) is, in my opinion, one of the most moving studies of a dog ever painted. Here Crawhall seems to enter into the very life and spirit of this sensitive, graceful creature, and every part is 'invoked' with consummate knowledge of its structure. 'Joe' Crawhall is one of the mysteries of the power of human intelligence. As a draughtsman, his method of working is beyond explanation, since he seldom drew direct from his models but would sit and look at them for half an hour or so, and so memorize them as to be able to transfer form and colour to paper in swift, irrevocable strokes of the brush. Concentration on any theme is, of course, essential to its realization, but Crawhall's concentration was of such an exceptional order as to defy analysis. His horses, dogs and birds seem to have been cast out of the crucible of a mind working at fiery heat. Most artists know how difficult it is to memorize sufficiently to reproduce the simplest thing in nature. Crawhall's memory was so potent and so exact that his merest note has the infallible accent of truth.

Some day Evelyn Cheston's landscapes will hang with those of her peers in the galleries of the world. A great, unknown artist and heroic character, she added her vivid style to the many represented in this book. She was gifted with the heart of the poet and the eye of the naturalist, and lived only for the expression of beauty. Confronted with her Devonshire scenes one experiences the feeling that one is actually there, standing in immense solitude under the illimitable vault of the sky. Like Collier, she suffered from poor health and painted with a rapidity and urgency apprehensive of 'Time's wingèd chariot hurrying near'. Evelyn Cheston seemed to divine all that was essential in landscape for the expression of her mood. Even had she wished to enter into the details of the scene she had no time to do this; and it is better so, for she sought and found the *genius loci* and was uncommonly rewarded by nature for her passionate devotion. Her summarizations, with brushes fully charged with tint and body-colour, are like songs of praise for the pageant of the seasons and life itself, all the more poignant in that her own hold on life was so fragile and precarious.

Sir William Russell Flint's *The Lake and Grotto* (page 175) has all the requisites of a fine water-colour—excellent drawing, atmospheric effect, and poetic sentiment. Few artists in the medium have so thoroughly explored its subtleties. He has added his own personality to the tradition. Sir William has the gift of seeing the scene, however complicated, as an entity, and his power of constructing it all of a piece, under any effect of light and colour, places him among great contemporaries. This synthesis can be achieved only by knowledge of all the parts and by the elimination of those details that tend to harass or conflict with the essential lines of composition and design. To know what to eliminate in order to simplify the truth of things is gained only by life-long discipline. Mind and hand must be tempered to the acutest point of understanding of the subject and must work together in exact harmony. In Sir William's work, it is a graceful mind that looks always for the inevitable dignity of the landscape, and a graceful hand that records the effect with a fluency unique among artists of our time.

The water-colours that I have specifically mentioned show immense variety of style, from the brilliant sketch to the highly finished performance. Most of the artists, past and present, conform to one or other of these styles or strike a happy medium between the extremes. Rapid and lucid interpretation of the subject, rather than detailed execution, results in more robust and original work, but the lively thread of tradition runs through the whole School. In considering influences, there is something of Francis Towne in Girtin's work, and both Girtin and the youthful Turner learned from Dayes, John Robert Cozens and other predecessors. John Varley, having assimilated prevailing styles and added a sentiment of Claude, Poussin and Richard Wilson, was well equipped to help his many gifted pupils. Varley's true genius was in teaching. His sympathy and generosity in imparting his knowledge were of incalculable value to professional and amateur alike. As Elizabeth Turner, one of Varley's pupils, wrote on October 5, 1822: 'Far from feeling any jealousy for himself in his art, Mr Varley possesses so high an opinion of its excellence and so true a desire for its extension, that, as Moses—solely earnest for the honour of his God—wished all the people to be prophets, so he would make everyone an artist and as good as himself.'[1]

The most creative mind among the many young men who studied with Varley was probably Samuel Palmer's; and he also learned from William Blake, not so much in a technical sense (Palmer was a far finer technician) but from Blake's noble sentiment and religious mind. In this respect, the young and the old man had much in common, and frequently talked about art as they walked from South Molton Street to Hampstead to visit John Linnell, who was to become Palmer's father-in-law.

United in their choice of subjects were Joshua Cristall, George Barret, Jun., and Francis Oliver Finch. Barret and Finch, particularly, excelled in combining nature with classical sentiment.

Cotman, sequestered in Norwich for the best part of his life, had little influence on his contemporaries in London; and it is the water-colourists of the present century who have felt the full impact of his genius. Mr Charles Knight, Mr Leonard Squirrell and Mr E. M. Dinkel perfectly understand his mood, and Mr Cecil Hunt is well aware of its profundity in mountain form.

De Wint, like Constable, is a permanent inspiration to landscape-painters. Whatever one's style one cannot but be instructed by de Wint's realistic breadth and atmospheric truth.

There is similarity between the drawings of Bonington, Boys and Callow. Their early work is not infrequently confused. Among the best draughtsmen of buildings today is Henry Rushbury, and though his way of drawing with the pen or pencil and tinting with delicate washes is personal, I do not doubt that he admires the urban scenes by Boys.

For high finish we have John Frederick Lewis, Frederick Walker, William Henry Hunt, Myles Birket Foster and W. J. Wainwright. Their styles differ from the earlier masters in that the piling of detail upon detail with the aid of body-colour restricts the easy flow of the wash, and approximates to an oil-painting technique. The fact that the effort is so prolonged produces

[1] Sydney D. Kitson, *Notes on a Collection of Portrait Drawings by Dawson Turner*. Walpole Society, Vol. XXI.

an elaborate result. Compare Birket Foster's *The Green Lane*, in which every fact is recorded, with the noble freedom of de Wint's *Valley of the Thames and Cliveden Woods*. I know of nobody today who is painting in this highly wrought method. Maybe this style is crystallized in its very conscientiousness, but Lewis and Walker were great artists. Hunt and Birket Foster had remarkable gifts, but tended to allow stippling and insistence on *minutiae* to limit their vision and imagination.

In compiling this book I had in mind the many degrees of taste in art, and I hope that every reader will find something that specially appeals to him.

Here is the world as our water-colourists see it, a world of beauty, whether in landscape, seascape, skyscape, figures, architecture or flowers. Here are the seasons—spring, summer, autumn and winter—unfolded for the delight of eye, heart and mind. The effort, the love and the idealism that have gone to the making of these drawings during the last two hundred years is a solemn thought in itself. They are but a modicum of innumerable and equally beautiful works. They are, I venture to say, very reflective of a highly cultured and progressive race.

The short life-histories enliven the personalities of the artists and record their contact with the world. Some are famous, some are obscure, some were lavishly rewarded for their pains, quite a few died in poverty. Among them are great figures like J. M. W. Turner, John Constable, David Wilkie, John Sargent and Wilson Steer. Some died very young, like Girtin and Bonington. Several were octogenarians, or older, like Cornelius Varley, William Callow and George Clausen. Ill-health did not prevent certain of this elect company from creating the masterpiece. At least three of them endured the worst disaster that can happen to an artist—increasing blindness. Two were killed in the second World War, dutifully recording that war, and one was destroyed by an enemy bomb at his home.

What of the future of water-colour painting? Is it capable of further development? The Old Masters, who had reached perfection over a hundred years ago, might well have asked the same question. Could they see what a wealth of exquisite drawings has been done since their time, they would be the first to admit that their art, like nature herself, is endowed with perennial youth. There is no mortgage on the inspired mind. It belongs to the eternal. Such fine art as this is part of our nation's destiny, and symbolical of our belief that life is a beautiful experience, however haunted it may be with conflict and perplexities.

ADRIAN BURY

ALEXANDER COZENS

c. 1717–86

ONE OF the most original landscape painters, Alexander Cozens was born in Russia. His somewhat mysterious youth gave rise to the legend that he was the son of Peter the Great by a Deptford woman whom Peter took to Russia with him. This has been disproved in recent years. Alexander's mother was a Mary Davenport who married Richard Cozens, a shipbuilder; they went to Russia at the Czar's request and lived in St Petersburg. Cozens studied in Italy (where he came under the influence of Claude), travelled to England, and worked as drawing master at Christ's Hospital, at Eton, and probably at Bath. During the last years of his life he was famous as a teacher in London, and was 'Instructor in Drawing to the Young Princes'. Cozens was full of theories and systems, and published books on how to draw trees and skies and *The Principles of Beauty Relative to the Human Head*: but his most interesting publication is his *New Method for Assisting the Invention in the Composition of Landscape*. Briefly, the idea was to stain the paper accidentally, and let the 'blot' suggest a landscape idea which the student could develop in a broad, free way without details. That it was immensely popular is proved by the fact that Edward Dayes, a drawing master in the old topographical tradition, dubbed Cozens 'Blotmaster to the Town'. Cozens came under the patronage of the fantastic and fabulously rich William Beckford of Fonthill, as did John Robert, his son. Both artists have had considerable influence on our water-colour painters. A small number of connoisseurs from the eighteenth century to the present day have always believed in Cozens' genius, but it was not until the exhibition at the Tate Gallery in December 1946 that the public were able to see as many as a hundred examples of his art. Thanks to Mr Paul Oppé's scholarly enthusiasm this exhibition was one of the events in the art world and definitely placed the genius of Cozens where it belonged, in the front rank of creative artists. It may be said that Cozens was one of the first artists in England to interpret the poetry of nature in terms both simple and profound.

LANDSCAPE WITH WOODED CRAG
Alexander Cozens

Signed on mount, Alexr. Cozens. Engraved in reverse in mezzotint by W. Pether, 1785, as plate 42 of the New Method, the second of the three finished compositions from the same blot (pl. 40).

By permission of Sir Edward Marsh, K.C.V.O.

[8½ × 11¾ in.]

PAUL SANDBY

R.A.

1725–1809

A T THE age of eighty Paul Sandby, ruminating in his house at St George's Row, near Tyburn, could remember a long and successful life in which he had played a dominant part in the eighteenth-century art world. Sandby hailed from Nottingham. At twenty-one he was in the Tower of London drawing office, and in the same year made a *Survey in the Highlands* and did many spirited drawings of Scottish town and country subjects. His brother, Thomas, had become draughtsman and secretary to the Duke of Cumberland, and having accompanied the Duke on all his campaigns was appointed Deputy Ranger of Windsor Great Park. Paul frequently visited his brother at Windsor, and here they seem to have led a happy and useful existence drawing Windsor and the vicinity, and designing Virginia Water. Paul was influential in founding the Society of Artists, and was later a foundation member of the Royal Academy. He was the first to practise the charming medium of aquatint which made it possible to reproduce tinted drawings with an almost facsimile effect. This process was brought to England from France by the Hon. Charles Greville. Paul Sandby's water-colours were often more than accomplished topographical drawings. If he did not touch the heights of poetic expression, he had a rare sense of landscape and was adept in enlivening the scene with figures, particularly equestrian ones, and pretty and graceful women. Friend and admirer of the great but neglected Richard Wilson, he endeavoured to sell some of the master's drawings, but failing to do so bought them himself. Sandby told Wilson that they had been sold to pupils. A forerunner of the school of water-colourists, he lived to see this English art evolve into 'something rich and strange'. A few doors away from him in St George's Row, young Tom Girtin had taken up the torch, lighting the way to a new world of beautiful expression, only to lay it down and die prematurely at twenty-seven, seven years before old Paul himself was laid to rest at the age of eighty-four. The drawings of Paul and Thomas Sandby are the only ones that have been consistently acquired for the Royal Collection from the dates of their death.

WINDSOR

PAUL SANDBY, R.A.

Signed P. Sandby, 1785. This view of Windsor is a 'free composition introducing Windsor Castle and Eton College in a mainly imaginary landscape'.

*Formerly in Mr F. J. Nettlefold's Collection and presented by him to the
Bowes Museum, County Durham.*

[11¾ × 17½ in.]

FRANCIS COTES
R.A.

1726–70

As a portrait artist, especially in pastels, Francis Cotes won considerable eminence. Though Hogarth exaggerated when he said that Cotes was a better painter than Reynolds, none the less there are works by Cotes —the portrait of Queen Charlotte with the Princess Royal on her lap, for instance, in the Duke of Northumberland's collection—which can be compared not unfavourably with Reynolds's best works. Son of an Irish apothecary, Cotes studied under Knapton, exhibited at the Society of Artists, and was a foundation member of the Royal Academy. Some of his portraits in pastels and oils are well known, but that he was an excellent draughtsman of landscape in water-colours is proved by the *Landscape with View of a Country Seat*, in the Victoria and Albert Museum. As this drawing is signed and dated 1750 it shows more skill and subtlety of tinting than we generally expect at so early a date. The subject is the typical country mansion with its parklands, but where it differs from other drawings of the period is in its fine realization of trees in the foreground, elegant figures sensitively drawn, and not over-emphasized architectural interest. Here is one of the earliest and best water-colour landscapes, a work of art rather than craft. If Cotes does not express the imaginative perception of Towne or Cozens, he certainly renders the scene with commendable technical skill and largeness of vision. Withal the design is arranged decoratively, and one feels the natural environment of this charmingly discreet country house. It is an interesting fact that Cotes was associated with Paul Sandby and painted his portrait. *Landscape with View of a Country Seat* has something of Paul Sandby's style, but has more delicacy of touch. Cotes worked in Bath and in London, and died at his house in Cavendish Square at the early age of forty-four.

LANDSCAPE WITH VIEW OF A COUNTRY SEAT

FRANCIS COTES, R.A.

Signed and dated 1750.

By permission of the Victoria and Albert Museum.

[14½ × 21⅛ in.]

31

FRANCIS TOWNE

c. 1740–1816

IT IS NOT uncommon for an artist, famous in his day, to sink into obscurity. If Francis Towne was never widely known, he was respected by certain contemporaries—John 'Warwick' Smith, William Pars, John Downman and others—but little did any of them think, not even Towne himself, perhaps, how justly deserving he was of a very high place in the English school of water-colour painting. It was not until Mr Paul Oppé revealed Towne's genius in the eighth volume of the Walpole Society (1920) that we were able to assess the value of his style, and its influence in the eighteenth century and the twentieth. Towne, born in the west country (the actual place is not known), studied at Shipley's School in London, lived and taught in the neighbourhood of Exeter, and made various tours of Wales, Italy and Switzerland. The words classic and romantic have been so bandied about as to have lost their meaning, but if to be classic is to be a master of form and to regard nature as a kind of architectural unity, Francis Towne had this gift *in excelsis*. It was the artist's love of form that made the monstrous, mouldering Roman monument irresistible to him. His drawings of the Colosseum and other antiquities have grandeur of vision, plus that essential austerity which was part of the Roman genius. As if to keep within the bounds of reason when surveying either the work of nature or of man, Towne uses the neatest of pen lines to hold everything together, as it were, in a certain linear restraint. An artist to whom the Colosseum was just a subject for drawing was not to be intimidated by the structural sublimities of the Alps, but in spite of his precise pen and brush strokes Towne had a sinewy sentiment. It is the sentiment that one feels in eighteenth-century poetry, such as that of Gray or Collins. Towne has a certain personal touch that entitles him to stand with the more creative water-colourists. He has some affinity with John Robert Cozens, though Towne's technique generally is more assured. His sense of colour and way of laying each tint are quite remarkable for grace of style. Towne exhibited at the Society of Artists, the Free Society, the Royal Academy, and the British Institution. His name and work had passed almost completely out of knowledge until about thirty years ago, since when he has become one of the 'darlings' of connoisseurs, and deservedly so, for his admirable technique and aristocratic mind.

NEAR NAPLES

FRANCIS TOWNE

Signed and dated F. Towne, delt. 1781. View on the side of a valley looking towards a hill with a distant glimpse of the Bay.

By permission of the British Museum.

[$12\frac{3}{4} \times 18\frac{1}{2}$ in.]

NICHOLAS POCOCK

1741–1821 ('Old Society')[1]

OF THE ten artists who met at the Stratford Coffee House in Oxford Road on November 30, 1804, to found the Society of Painters in Water-Colours, Nicholas Pocock was the oldest. In fact, he was forty years older than the youngest 'conspirator', Cornelius Varley, who was just twenty-three. Pocock was already famous as a delineator of ships. His water-colours form an important record of naval events at the end of the eighteenth and the beginning of the nineteenth centuries. Pocock was a sea captain himself and thus had a sailor's knowledge of all kinds of craft. During his leisure moments afloat and ashore he expressed a strong natural talent for drawing. His earliest known work is the *Illustrated Log* of his voyage to Jamaica in 1776. Precisely when he retired from the sea is not known; but it is possible that he was present at Lord Howe's victory of the Glorious First of June 1794, judging by the actuality of four sketches of that action. Certain it is that Pocock became famous for pictures of naval encounters exhibited at the 'Old Society', the Royal Academy, and the British Institution. Many of these were founded on information given and sketches lent to him, by serving officers. They were accompanied by spirited and exact descriptions of the engagement in question, such as: 'Lord Howe's Victory over the French Fleet on the 1st of June 1794, taken at half-past ten o'clock, Forenoon, when the Queen Charlotte passed through the Enemy's Line, and was hawling upon the lee-quarter of the Montague, whose fire she had totally silenced.' Much of his art is devoted to naval affairs, but Pocock was also a good topographer and could limn the country mansion with the expert touch. Although he was celebrated for many years and lived to the age of eighty little about his personality has come down to us. As Randall Davies wrote in the *Old Water-Colour Society's Club*, Volume V (1927–8), ' he is perhaps the only artist of whom there is not a single anecdote'. He was born in Bristol, son of Nicholas Pocock, a Bristol merchant, lived in Great George Street, Westminster, and died at Ray Lodge, Maidenhead, March 9, 1821.

[1] I use the expression 'Old Society' for those artists who were members of the Society of Painters in Water-Colours before it assumed the prefix 'Royal' on July 20, 1881.

LLANSTEPHAN CASTLE, COAST OF CARMARTHENSHIRE

NICHOLAS POCOCK

By permission of the Victoria and Albert Museum.

[14¾ × 20⅝ in.]

35

MICHAEL 'ANGELO' ROOKER

A.R.A.

1743–1801

Rooker came of age at a time of the awakening of landscape art in England. Richard Wilson, George Lambert and George Barret, Sen., the Smiths of Chichester and Wright of Derby, were doing excellent work in the oil medium, while Paul Sandby was showing the way in the water-colour method. It was a fortunate chance that Rooker, son of an engraver, went to Sandby for lessons in the topographical style of drawing. Sandby nicknamed Rooker 'Angelo', and the pupil was not unworthy of the master's playful humour, for he soon showed his mettle at the Society of Artists' exhibitions in 1763, 1765 and 1768. He followed Wilson and Sandby into the Royal Academy when this institution was founded in 1768, and exhibited there. Rooker was also an engraver of distinction, but an interesting departure from graver and brush was his term of office at the Haymarket Theatre as principal scene painter; and, since it was a public whim to think that Italian names were indispensable to art, Michael 'Angelo' Rooker became, for the nonce, 'Signor Rookerini', and felt presumably more at home with Zuccarelli, Cipriani and all the rest of them. Among the first to make those tours of England in search of antiquities for pencil and water-colour, he was a subtle draughtsman of picturesque ruins, such as *Boxgrove Priory Church, near Chichester*; *St. Botolph's Priory, Colchester*; and *Llanthony Abbey*—all enlivened with charming little figures. His tree-drawing also showed great skill. Though his style was not unlike that of his master, Paul Sandby, Rooker had his own delicacy of touch and tint. He could work, if necessary, on a small scale. In the Victoria and Albert Museum there are six illustrations, no larger than $5\frac{1}{8}$ by $2\frac{3}{4}$ inches, to Fielding's stories.

BOXGROVE PRIORY CHURCH, NEAR CHICHESTER

MICHAEL 'ANGELO' ROOKER, A.R.A.

By permission of the Victoria and Albert Museum.

[11 × 14¾ in.]

JOHN 'WARWICK' SMITH

1749–1831 ('Old Society')

S ON OF a gardener, John 'Warwick' Smith was a typical product of the age of patronage. He first came under the notice of Captain John Bernard Gilpin, father of two successful artists, and was introduced by Gilpin to Sir Harry Harper. At Harper's house, the second Earl of Warwick (1746–1816), himself an amateur artist, was so impressed by Smith's talents that he offered to send him to Italy. Whether the Earl accompanied Smith is doubtful, but the fact remains that the artist studied there for five years at the Earl's expense. On his return he married, settled down at Warwick, contributed to Middieman's *Select Views,* and published drawings of Italy and Wales, and *Views of the Lakes*. His place as an artist was secure long before the founding of the Society of Painters in Water-Colours in 1804. He joined it in 1805, exhibiting regularly, and becoming its President on three occasions, 1819, 1821, and 1823. In 1823 his drawing of the Colosseum was regarded by Sir George Beaumont as the 'best in the room'. He had in the meantime moved to London, living successively at St George's Row, Oxford Street, and Bryanston Street, Portman Square. Though he comes into the era of topographical artists, Smith had creative abilities far beyond the mere recording of places, and frequently took liberties with his subject to express a poetic effect. Though Girtin and Turner are credited with having transformed the topographical drawing into a work of real art rather than craft, Smith had long expressed, both in colour and design, the richer possibilities of the water-colour medium. It is likely that he was influenced by Francis Towne, with whom Smith travelled from Italy to Switzerland in 1781, but his own individuality is such that his work has not only a definite style, but was far more pregnant for the advancement of the water-colour school than is generally realized. The *Temple of the Sibyl, Tivoli*, is a noble work. The facts of architecture and of nature, the light, shade and atmosphere are summarized with the certainty of genius.

TEMPLE OF THE SIBYL, TIVOLI
John 'Warwick' Smith

By permission of the National Gallery of Canada, Ottawa.
[$20\frac{11}{16} \times 13\frac{15}{16}$ in.]

JOHN ROBERT COZENS

1752–99

'Cozens was all poetry, and your drawing is a lovely specimen,' wrote John Constable to Archdeacon Fisher on August 4, 1821. Thus, over a hundred and twenty years ago, Cozens was recognized by one of the world's greatest landscape painters. Such was the highest praise he could receive; nor did he fail of appreciation in his lifetime. Son of Alexander Cozens, John studied under his father, exhibited when he was fifteen, and travelled at twenty-four to Switzerland with the celebrated connoisseur, Richard Payne Knight, for whom he did a series of somewhat immature drawings. His second Continental tour was made in company with William Beckford of *Vathek* fame. They set out in May 1782. 'The party travelled in princely state; in the first carriage were Beckford and his ex-tutor, in the second, Cozens and a musician, Mr Burton,' and the usual retinue of servants. A truly grand tour which ended for Cozens at Rome. He is playing the violoncello to Sir William Hamilton at Naples in 1783, 'as indolent as ever', so Sir William writes. The fact is that Cozens worked by fits and starts, but was always dreaming of the pictures he would eventually do from memory and rough notes. He achieved a large number. It is neither in quantity nor technique that his water-colours command respect, but in the artist's distinction of mind, the profound melancholy and austere grandeur that haunt his scenes. Some of his drawings are overpowering in their intensity of feeling. Was this fine mind stricken by the weight of its contemplation? It began to fail about 1792, and he died insane in December 1799. In their learned survey of Cozens's life and work, published by the Walpole Society, Volume XXIII (1934–5), Messrs C. F. Bell and Thomas Girtin state that the place of the artist's death is not recorded, 'but it was almost certainly the historic mansion called Brooke House, Clapton, which has been for much more than a century, and still is, a private hospital for mental patients'. Dr Thomas Monro, friend and patron of Cozens, was in charge of this asylum at the time. It was Monro who introduced the young Girtin and Turner to Cozens's work, and, copying it, they were to some extent influenced by it.

VIEW IN THE ISLAND OF ELBA

JOHN ROBERT COZENS

Signed and dated 1780 (?).

By permission of the Victoria and Albert Museum.

$[14\frac{1}{2} \times 21\frac{1}{8} \text{ in.}]$

FRANCIS NICHOLSON

1753–1844 ('OLD SOCIETY')

LIVING till the age of ninety-one, painting to the end, and still vigorous in intellect, as witness his last correspondence, Francis Nicholson had watched the evolution and triumph of our school of water-colour painters. He had, in fact, done much to enlarge its scope. Convinced that the method was capable of richer colour effect, that it was possible to render light by allowing the paper to suggest it, he had produced work that had an important influence on the younger men, including even Turner. In Nicholson's youth the usual practice was to cover the paper with a general tint, increasing the darks, and adding the darkest part last. Nicholson reversed the process, 'stopping out the lights' and thereby giving transparency and brilliance to such parts as needed them. He had already gained a reputation for this 'invention' before he came to London, for a story is told that the Earl of Warwick confounded an artist-friend, who remarked that it was impossible to get the brilliance of water without the use of body-colour, by showing him some of Nicholson's drawings. Born at Pickering in Yorkshire, Nicholson as a boy suffered the conventional parental opposition, but prevailed upon his father to allow him to study. At the early age of sixteen he set up as an artist at Pickering, painting portraits, horses, dogs and dead game. After the age of thirty he lived for some years at Whitby, with occasional visits to London, but in 1804 we find him among the foundation-members of the 'Old Society', and a successful drawing-master in Charlotte Street, Fitzroy Square. Nicholson sold his works to the connoisseurs of the day, including Lord Mulgrave, the Earl of Warwick, Lord Bute, Sir Richard Colt Hoare and Walter Fawkes. He exhibited at the 'Old Society' from 1805 to 1813, when he retired, but sent eleven works to the exhibition of 1815, after which his name no longer appears in the catalogues. As a painter of rocky scenery, and especially of moving water, Nicholson takes a high place. He was scientifically minded, and studied mechanics, optics and chemistry. He was also a musician and could build an organ with his own hands.

THE DRIPPING ROCK

Francis Nicholson

By permission of Mrs I. J. Dunne.
[12 × 16½ in.]

THOMAS ROWLANDSON

1756–1827

THERE is no artist quite like Tom Rowlandson. His gay, gallant, humorous, reckless, sensitive nature is inscribed all over his work. As an interpreter of the reason and unreason of the eighteenth and early nineteenth centuries Rowlandson is unique, and if all other records were lost we could well read in his drawings the full-blooded pageant of life as our ancestors knew it from 1770 to 1827. Rowlandson is a veritable encyclopædia of the follies, vices, wit and elegance of Georgian England. A London cockney, the artist was born the son of a tradesman in Old Jewry, and the carillon of Bow Church would appear to have rung all the changes on his heart and mind. His career began at Barrow's Academy in Soho Square, but we find him, at the age of sixteen, in Paris on a visit to an indulgent French aunt who had married his uncle. In 1775, trying his hand at portraiture, Rowlandson exhibited at the Royal Academy, and his address at that time was in Wardour Street. It was not long, however, before he discovered his true genius for drawing spontaneously with the pen and tinting his works with appropriate washes of colour. The money he received for them was supplemented by a legacy of £7000, no small fortune in the eighteenth century. The same aunt who had befriended him in his 'teens left him this sum, and other property, which he speedily squandered in gambling. Rowlandson, the artist, was also the great gamester, and he would wager a fortune on cards, winning or losing with imperturbability. It is said that he once sat playing at the card-table for thirty-six hours on end. Losing everything, he merely remarked, holding up his pencil, 'I've played the fool, but here is my resource'. The strange thing about Rowlandson is that in spite of his love of pleasure he did acres of work. For a long time he was regarded only as a caricaturist, but recent criticism and research have placed his reputation on a deservedly higher basis. He had a rare sense of beauty and was a landscape artist of much skill. Mr F. Gordon Roe's book, published in 1947, gives the liveliest picture of this most ingenious, imaginative, and technically brilliant son of the eighteenth century.

STROLLING PLAYER

THOMAS ROWLANDSON

By permission of Mrs I. J. Dunne.
[5¼ × 5¼ in.]

45

WILLIAM BLAKE

1757–1827

IF ROWLANDSON was the designer of the world and the flesh, Blake was the designer of the spirit. In the firmament of poetry and painting Blake is a lone star of exceptional brilliance, the isolated visionary and mystic for whom the ideal was the real. Blake's life is epitomized in the remark he made when a child that he had seen a 'tree full of angels', for indeed he went about seeing what others would or could not see. He was not among those who 'put away childish things', so-called; for with Blake the child was father to the man, and he tried to live his life like one of his own *Songs of Innocence*. It is not to be wondered at that he who thought so little of this world was thought little of *by* the world in which he had his corporeal being. However comforted by spectral visitants, or encouraged and supported by such friends as Hayley, Flaxman, Linnell, the Varleys and Palmer, Blake must have been fully aware that poverty was his destined lot and that his dreams and visions were not really for sale. Yet truly they had to be sold in order to pay the common bills of daily living. Nor need we assume that he was unable to defend himself against the 'slings and arrows of outrageous fortune', as witness some of his letters, particularly the one in which he disproves the false accusation made by a drunken soldier that he had uttered seditious remarks. In days when the law of libel hardly applied, Blake's work so annoyed some of the critics that he was called a 'madman' in print; but he persisted in his way, on the arm of his devoted wife, and probably found far greater happiness than mountains of gold could buy. It has remained for the twentieth century to make a profitable corner in Blake, and I do not doubt that the poet-painter would have been amazed at the machinations of Mammon in this respect. His work, like that of all true genius, is beyond price, but it is an ironical thought that the present cost of one of his drawings would have supported Blake in comparative luxury for years. His influence on the rising generation of painters and poets—Palmer, Linnell, Calvert and some of the pre-Raphaelites—was profound. Blake may be said to have been one of the holy men of art, and to have waged a holy war against all that was mean, sordid and abominable in the world. He is a voice crying in the wilderness.

SATAN AROUSING THE REBEL ANGELS
WILLIAM BLAKE

Milton. *Paradise Lost*. Book 1, 299-303.

By permission of the Victoria and Albert Museum.
[20¼ × 15⅜ in.]

47

DR THOMAS MONRO

1759–1833

A CHARMING character in British art was Dr Thomas Monro. He might be called the godfather of water-colour painters. A distinguished physician, and one who was called in on attendance to George III, Monro was never happier than when sketching or helping others to sketch. His chief claim to fame is in the encouragement he gave to the younger generation, many of them boys of great talent. Discussing Monro in the *Old Water-Colour Society's Club,* Volume II (1924–5), the late Very Reverend W. Foxley Norris, D.D., wrote: 'As I think of my great-grandfather, then I seem to see a kindly, hospitable man who loved beauty for its own sake, and cared not a jot whether the friends and disciples with whom he surrounded himself were well or humbly born so long as they too could show a love for beauty and pursue art with reverence and determination.' This is a truly aristocratic attitude, and from such a sentiment all the culture in the world has derived. Monro was always on the alert for genius in need of spiritual and material comfort. If we could re-create an evening at his town house in Adelphi Terrace we would see 'the good Dr' surrounded by aspiring boys who were to write their names across the firmament of immortality. Here is a grand constellation! —J. M. W. Turner, Thomas Girtin, John Varley, W. H. Hunt, John Linnell, Copley Fielding, Peter de Wint. He was sufficiently accomplished an artist himself to instruct them, but they also learned much from his collection of drawings and paintings by the great English and continental masters. We hear that these 'Bohemian' gatherings were not always 'popular in the family, for some of the young men were rough diamonds, notably Turner. . . . Mrs Monro was inclined to retire into her shell, and to have her dinner upstairs, and great-aunt Sally complain of this unseemly invasion of the house'. But Dr Monro didn't care. His name survives agreeably associated with one of the great movements in art. Not only for that, but for the generous way in which he looked after his protégés, introducing them to collectors, helping them by buying their drawings, and tending the older artists in sickness.

LANDSCAPE WITH RIVER
DR THOMAS MONRO

Adrian Bury's Collection.
[5½ × 8½ in.]

JULIUS CAESAR IBBETSON

1759–1817

THE LIFE of Ibbetson would confirm the idea that man is born to trouble, as the sparks fly upward. His birth resulted in the death of his mother, the nineteen-year-old girl whom Ibbetson, senior, a man of over fifty, had married against local hostility. The artist-to-be was brought into this world by means of a caesarean operation, and this fact is 'recorded' in his second name. Sent to schools at Fulneck and Leeds, Ibbetson was so decidedly talented in the direction of drawing that he was apprenticed in due time to a ship-painter, but one whose work had utilitarian rather than artistic interest. Ibbetson revolted against this and ran away to London. Here, at least, he was able to see pictures, and to 'pot-boil' for dealers. He first exhibited at the Royal Academy at the age of twenty-six, but, having married some years previously, Ibbetson found it difficult to provide for his increasing family. Perhaps for this reason he accepted a 'safe' post (as he thought) as draughtsman to Colonel Cathcart's embassy to China. The mission failed, however, owing to Cathcart's death at Java, and Ibbetson wasted a year, receiving no remuneration. Some patronage from the Marquess of Bute and the Hon. Wilbraham Tollemache was of use; but the death of Ibbetson's wife reduced him to a state of despair. Death seems to have haunted this unfortunate man, for eight of his eleven children had preceded their mother to the grave. We find Ibbetson consoling himself with boon companions, such as George Morland,[1] in the taverns of the town, and no doubt gathering material there for jolly pictures like *A Married Sailor's Return* and *An Unmarried Sailor's Return*, lately in the Nettlefold Collection and given by Mr Nettlefold to the Tate Gallery. Always in debt, Ibbetson was always on the look-out for a patron or dealer who would relieve him of financial worries. One such called Thomas Vernon offered hope. He would discharge Ibbetson's debts in payment for pictures to be painted. The artist carried out his part of the contract, but Vernon went bankrupt, leaving Ibbetson still further embarrassed. Fate, however, made amends at last. A well-to-do patron, William Danby of Swinton Park, Yorkshire, provided the artist with a house at Masham, and here with his second wife, children and grandchildren, he found peace.

[1] Samuel and Richard Redgrave affirm that Ibbetson and Morland were friends; but Miss Rotha Mary Clay, in her life of *Julius Caesar Ibbetson* (1949), quotes from a letter to the effect that Ibbetson neither liked nor trusted Morland.

THE MARKET
JULIUS CAESAR IBBETSON

By permission of the Laing Art Gallery, Newcastle-upon-Tyne.
[8½ × 11½ in.]

EDWARD DAYES

1763–1804

IT WAS unfortunate for Edward Dayes's memory that some manuscript notes by him on his contemporaries were published posthumously,[1] for they reveal him to have been a somewhat embittered and unreliable character, as was only too tragically confirmed by his suicide in 1804. His animadversions on Thomas Girtin, his pupil of genius, have been proved to be without foundation. The probability is that he was jealous of Girtin's superior talents. When the younger artist rebelled against being used as drudge to colour prints Dayes is said to have had him imprisoned in the Fleet as a refractory apprentice. The legend continues that Girtin covered the walls of his cell with such wonderful drawings that the Earl of Essex bought up the indentures, burnt them in the presence of Girtin, and took the young artist to Cassiobury, his Hertfordshire 'palace', and allowed him to work as he wished. Nor is it forgotten that Dayes, obviously out of pique, called Alexander Cozens 'Blotmaster to the Town'. Such anecdotes have tended to obscure the considerable talents of one of our early water-colourists. The more one looks at Dayes's work, the more convinced one is that he was a fine draughtsman of architecture and figures. Withal, one feels that his accomplishment was acquired with great and untiring effort, the work of a man who did not find it easy to draw, and was perhaps as unattractive to society as Cozens and Girtin were popular. I submit that both Girtin and Turner in their youth were much indebted to Dayes. Dr Monro, mentor of many young water-colourists, had a large number of Dayes's drawings in his collection. The style of the fine *The Priory Church, Tynemouth*, in the Laing Collection, Newcastle-upon-Tyne, is not only echoed in some of Turner's and Girtin's early architectural drawings, but is also an excellent lesson for any student of the medium. It has become fashionable in these days of shoddy, surrealistic craftsmanship to dismiss the topographical school as uninspired and unimaginative, but it is the basis of much good water-colour painting.

[1] *The Works of Edward Dayes, with illustrative Notes by E. W. Brayley*, 1805.

THE PRIORY CHURCH, TYNEMOUTH
Edward Dayes

Engraved in Britton's *Architectural Antiquities of Great Britain*, 1813,
Vol. IV, p. 110, Plate 11.

By permission of the Laing Art Gallery, Newcastle-upon-Tyne.
[19¾ × 14⅝ in.]

GEORGE BARRET, Jun.

c. 1767–1842 ('Old Society')

ONE OF the foundation members of the 'Old Society', George Barret is remembered for his broad and truthful morning and evening effects, such being his favourite times for sketching landscape. He would go to the same spot over and over again, make quick notes of the subject and compose his drawings in the studio. A conscientious artist, he thought much more of his work than the money he might receive for it. Roget informs us that 'he had continued, as indeed he did to the end, to wrestle with poverty; but, while working thriftily to support a wife and family, he ever thought more of putting gold into his drawings than of the amount of the precious metal for which those drawings might be exchanged'. His work suggests something of the serenity of Richard Wilson's sunset glow, and it is an interesting fact that George Barret's father, also a landscape painter, was Wilson's immensely successful rival. George Barret, Jun., owing to his father's improvidence, had to begin to earn his living very early. In spite of the economic pressure Barret did a great deal of work, exhibiting no less than 581 water-colours at the 'Old Society', five at the Royal Academy, nineteen at the British Institution and eight at Suffolk Street (the Society of British Artists). His *Theory and Practice of Water-Colour Painting*, published in 1840, is still of interest to students. For a long time Barret resided at 17 Devonshire Place, Edgware Road, a neighbourhood then remote from town. Indeed, he would advise his pupils to watch the sunsets over the Paddington Canal from the bridge at Maida Hill. The place has long been completely urbanized, though a modern artist, Mr Algernon Newton, R.A., has revealed the beauty that is still to be seen along these London waterways. Barret is buried in the old churchyard of St Mary's, Paddington Green, a place known to him from childhood to old age. It was the subject of his last drawing, accompanied by four lines of verse entitled *Thoughts in a Churchyard*.

MALHAM COVE
GEORGE BARRET, JUN.

By permission of the Victoria and Albert Museum.

[17¾ × 24½ in.]

55

JOSHUA CRISTALL

1767–1847 ('Old Society')

Of the 358 works exhibited by Joshua Cristall at the 'Old Society' during his forty-two years' association with that body, the majority are figure subjects in landscape backgrounds. Not a few are entitled Pastorals. Some are founded on the poetry of Virgil, Ovid, Theocritus, Shakespeare and Milton. Though not a classical scholar, Cristall possessed the classical temperament, and it is greatly to his credit that, in spite of handicaps and lack of encouragement in early life and manhood, he acquired all the learning necessary to fulfil his classical sense of beauty. Before he could devote himself to art, Cristall had to waste many years trying to earn a living in uncongenial commercial work. For a time he was a student under James Barry at the Royal Academy Schools, and doubtless from that turbulent master of figure-painting he acquired uncommon power of delineation. But at twenty-six he is still employed 'at Mr Turner's China Manufactory, near Broseley, Salop', judging by letters he received there from Mary Wollstonecraft. He had sought her advice, but the pompous and patronizing tone of these letters must have brought little comfort to the aspiring artist. One of them concludes on this note: 'If you cannot bear some present inconvenience you are a common man, and will never rise to any degree of eminence in anything you undertake.' In point of fact Cristall did rise in time to such a degree of eminence as to be one of the foundation members and President of the Society of Painters in Water-Colours. Such success, however, that he achieved against life-long difficulties was a *succès d'estime* rather than one of monetary value. Is it possible that Cristall was too realistic in his figures and too idealistic in his backgrounds to appeal to the popular mind? There is no certain accounting for the fact that some artists carry off all the rewards in life while others, equally gifted, fail to win a competence. Cristall died poor, as he had lived, at the age of eighty. The sale of his remaining works at Christie's on April 11, 12, and 13, 1848, makes a pathetic commentary on Cristall's efforts. The 617 lots, which may easily have amounted to about two thousand drawings, fetched a total of £185 13s.

CLASSICAL LANDSCAPE WITH FIGURES

JOSHUA CRISTALL

By permission of Mrs I. J. Dunne.

[19¼ × 26 in.]

57

JOHN GLOVER

1767–1849 ('Old Society')

IMAGINE a tall, club-footed young man, eighteen stone in weight, wandering about the Leicestershire fields during leisure from agricultural work studying nature and taming wild birds so that they would come and go at his call. Such was Glover. He had so beautiful a handwriting that he was appointed writing-master at Appleby Free School. He then discovered a talent for drawing country houses, and after nine lessons from William Payne and John Smith set up as a drawing-master in Lichfield. As time went on the career of the erstwhile rustic was literally paved with gold. At the end of the eighteenth century Glover and J. M. W. Turner would appear to have been running neck and neck for fame and money. The Lichfield drawing-master settled at 3 Montagu Square in 1805, and within a year he had sold drawings to the value of seven hundred guineas, and his prices for teaching rose to five guineas a day, or two guineas for a lesson of three hours. Carriages of the nobility and gentry congested Manchester Square, where he had bought a house. Everybody wanted to learn 'how to do it' from John Glover. He also had a property in the Lake District, which he sold in order to acquire a picture by Claude. In Paris in 1814 the artist painted a picture which he exhibited at the Salon. It so impressed the authorities that Louis XVIII 'ordered a gold medal to be struck in its honour'. 'This was prevented by the return of Napoleon, who, however, also admired the picture and sent it with a medal to England, whither Glover had already fled. It might be thought that Glover, so singularly fortunate, would be content to settle down in his old age and enjoy the fruits of his luck and industry, leaving to his numerous progeny the wealth that he had acquired. Glover, however, had the *wanderlust*, and at about the age of sixty-five he sold all his finished water-colours, many of his oil paintings, and his house in Manchester Square, and departed for Australia with four sons and a daughter and sixty thousand pounds. He bought a sheep farm in Tasmania and lived there like a Biblical patriarch, surrounded by descendants, dying at the age of eighty-two on December 9, 1849.

BORROWDALE
JOHN GLOVER

By permission of the Laing Art Gallery, Newcastle-upon-Tyne.

[16½ × 24 in.]

ROBERT HILLS

1769–1844 ('Old Society')

WHEN Robert Hills attended that momentous meeting at the Stratford Coffee House, Oxford Road, in November 1804, a meeting that was to result in the foundation of the Water-Colour Society, he was thirty-five. He had been engaged on a series of etchings of animals, 780 of which were published between 1798 and 1817. Hills was the thoroughly efficient artist, like so many of the water-colourists of that time, whose names are taken for granted until we begin carefully to study their works. He had amazing skill as a draughtsman of animals, and would stalk a stag for miles in order to make notes of its characteristics. His preliminary pencil drawings are perfect. Nor do the animals which he put into his landscapes lose in vitality from elaboration and detail. There is something rather Dutch about Hills's mood: it is so deliberate. His trees remind one of the Dutch landscapists. If they are perhaps a little too highly wrought for the water-colour method, they do prove that Hills was no stranger to hard work, and did not rely only upon a very pleasant instinct for arrangement and design. The artist lived through the heyday of the water-colour movement, and was the first secretary of the 'Old Society'. So popular was he with the members that they voted him a presentation of plate in 1809 to the value of a hundred guineas. Hills remained faithful to the Society throughout its early nineteenth-century vicissitudes, and acted in some official capacity or other for nearly forty years. He worked for the most part in England and Scotland, with occasional visits to Normandy. Perhaps his most exciting adventure was a visit to the battlefield of Waterloo a few weeks after the defeat of Napoleon. Captain Bruce Ingram possesses some of the drawings he made at that time, including *The Barn at La Haye Sainte* and *In Ysselmonde, Charloos*. The artist's experiences were published in 1816 under the title of *Sketches in Flanders and Holland; with some Account of a Tour through parts of those countries, shortly after the Battle of Waterloo; in a Series of Letters to a Friend*.

DEER IN A LANDSCAPE
ROBERT HILLS

[20⅛ × 16⅛ in]

HUGH WILLIAM WILLIAMS
(CALLED 'GRECIAN' WILLIAMS)

1773–1829

LITTLE-KNOWN today but very successful in his time was Hugh William Williams, whose sobriquet 'Grecian' identifies this artist with the subjects he painted. The interest in Graeco-Roman antiquities which prompted so many cultured Englishmen and artists to make the grand tour was his dominant inspiration. Ten years before the birth of Williams, Pars had gone to Greece, having been selected by the Dilettanti Society as draughtsman to Chandler and Revett, the archaeologists. Their combined work did much to stimulate the increasing enthusiasm for the glory that was Greece and the grandeur that was Rome. Hugh Williams was born in Wales, but early in life settled in Edinburgh. Scotland, in fact, became his adopted country. He began by making topographical drawings, and six large engravings of Highland Views published in 1811–12 contributed to his fame. Trying to enlarge his reputation in the south he was a candidate in 1808 for the Society of Painters in Water-Colours, but failing election he joined the rival, if short-lived, organization known as the Associated Artists in Water-Colours. Williams travelled for several years in Greece, and on his return to Edinburgh published the result of his tours and exhibited his drawings. His *Travels in Italy and Greece* (and the Ionian Islands) appeared in 1820; his *Views of Greece* came out in numbers between 1827 and 1829. The drawing of Thebes, on the opposite page, is very dignified and rich in colour, as well as being in a perfect state of preservation.

THEBES

HUGH WILLIAM WILLIAMS

By permission of Mrs I. J. Dunne.

$[19\frac{1}{4} \times 27 \text{ in.}]$

63

THOMAS HEAPHY

1775–1855 ('Old Society', Society of Artists)

WHETHER it was the Pre-Raphaelite mood, the Greenery-Yallery School, or the exotics of the 'nineties that suggested the effeminacy of painting and artists we are not prepared to argue, but reference to the biographical sketches in this book proves that painters, if necessary, have been as daring and pugnacious as anybody else; and Thomas Heaphy, like John Varley, was an exceptionally virile and audacious personality. Of Huguenot descent, he was born in Spitalfields, and fought his way out of his environment and apprenticeship to become a power in art. As a student at the Royal Academy he rebelled against the curriculum, and was always critical of this institution. Heaphy earned a living, at first, as a portrait painter, using his attractive wife as a model, but made a name by genre pictures in the manner of Wilkie and Mulready. Why the usually discerning W. H. Pyne in the *Somerset House Gazette* should have regarded them as vulgar is beyond our experience of these water-colours. Like Rowlandson, Heaphy depicted life as he saw it, with an emphasis occasionally on the beauty of women and children, however humble their stations. *Fisherman's Cottage* would appear to be an idealization of humanity, and we would be the last to pretend with our reformers of today that everything that happened before their advent was necessarily dark, squalid and barbarous. Even a fisherman's cottage in the early eighteen hundreds might have been a happy place. Heaphy's most famous picture is *The Fish Market, Hastings,* which was sold for over four hundred guineas. But after varying success the artist is finding the life of the studio too uneventful and is accompanying the British army fighting in Spain, living the life of the troops in most of the important battles, and painting portraits of the officers. These works are in the National Portrait Gallery. On his return to England, Heaphy completed a large study of the Duke of Wellington and his staff, helped to create the Society of British Artists, of which he was first President in 1823, and joined the New Society of Painters in Water-Colours in 1831. He had belonged to the 'Old Society' from 1807 to 1812. In spite of all these activities he found time to become an expert stone-quarrier, construct a pleasure-boat, build a house, invent an improved axle, and lay down a railway. Certainly, a forceful personality.

FISHERMAN'S COTTAGE
THOMAS HEAPHY

By permission of the Laing Art Gallery, Newcastle-upon-Tyne.
[18½ × 24½ in.]

JOHN CONSTABLE

R.A.

1776–1837

IN THE literature of art there is nothing more moving than John Constable's letters to his wife. In one dated May 1819 he writes, while on a short visit to Bergholt: 'Everything seems full of blossom of some kind, and at every step I take, and on whatever object I turn my eyes, that sublime expression of the Scriptures, "I am the resurrection and the life", seems as if uttered near me.' Truly, in Constable's pictures there is a mystical, luminous quality which could have come only from an artist who could also write, 'I thank God daily for a thousand blessings which I enjoy . . .' He was able to respond to those blessings and to make them the subject of gratitude in his work. Constable was always looking in reverence at simple things. 'From my window where I am now writing, I see all those sweet fields that once saw us so happy.' He was never tired of extolling the joys of nature. 'Nothing can exceed the beautiful appearance of the Country at this time; its freshness, its amenity . . .' The range of his mind places Constable among the great poets of nature, whether he depicts a vast, tumultuous sky in brave strokes of the brush, or draws some minute detail of leaf or tree with the pencil. It is that very awareness in Constable, that never-ceasing wonder at the miracle of creation that makes his work so convincing. 'How much I wish I had been with you on your fishing excursion in the New Forest!' he writes to his great friend, Archdeacon Fisher. 'What river can it be? But the sound of water escaping from mill-dams, etc., willows, old rotten planks, slimy posts, and brickwork, I love such things . . .' With a certain East Anglian doggedness Constable continued to paint as he saw and as he felt, undeterred by 'learned' criticism or public indifference. 'My art flatters nobody by *imitation*, it courts nobody by *smoothness*, it tickles nobody by *petiteness*, it is without either *fal de lal* or *fiddle de dee*, how can I hope to be popular?' Such sincerity, however, has had its reward in the world's increasing admiration since his day. Let us not talk of monetary values. Such are the machinations of the business mind. The fact that a Constable sold in 1944 for nearly fifty thousand pounds does not make it a better picture than it was when it left the artist's easel. Only the melancholy reflection remains that had Constable been without private means we should have been the poorer by many masterpieces.

OLD SARUM

JOHN CONSTABLE, R.A.

Presumably the drawing exhibited at the Royal Academy in 1834.

By permission of the Victoria and Albert Museum.

[11½ × 19 in.]

JOHN VARLEY

1778—1842 ('OLD SOCIETY')

HERE is one of the great eccentrics in the annals of British art—painter, astrologer and inventor. His life reads like an *extravaganza*. The death of his father left Varley, born of what were once regarded as gentlefolk, poor but free—free from his projected apprenticeship to a silversmith, since the father died before the boy could be bound. He determined to follow his own star, and developed so rapidly as a landscape-painter that he was famous before he was twenty-five. He exhibited regularly at the R.A. from the age of seventeen. At twenty-seven he helped to found the Society of Painters in Water-Colours. He married and became father of a growing family; his house in Old Broad Street, London, was always crowded with pupils, boys like John Linnell, F. O. Finch, William Henry Hunt, and William Turner (of Oxford), and older students like David Cox and Copley Fielding. Varley controlled this water-colour academy, a veritable seminary of genius, with a heart of gold—and a handy ruler lest the young students should waste their time in skylarking. In the great houses of the West End and in many a country mansion, Varley attended the nobility and gentry, teaching them the rudiments of water-colouring. It is said that he made three thousand a year in this way; but he was never able to control his finances. Often victimized by rogues, he gave away his money in handfuls, an improvidence that led him to the debtors' prison, which during the last years of his life was his second home. He was fanatically devoted to the 'science' of astrology, and daily followed the stellar influence on his life. Aware that something evil portended, he stayed at home, on one occasion, lest an accident befell him in the street. There was a cry of 'Fire!' Varley noticed smoke coming into the room. He made a few hurried notes about the planet that afflicted him, and removed himself to safety. Copley Fielding, meeting Varley some days afterwards, expressed the hope that the trouble, of which he had heard rumours, was not serious. Varley merely replied: 'No, only the house burnt down, I knew something would happen.' So many of Varley's predictions came true that he was as famous as a 'prophet' as he was as an artist. He married twice, had nine children, exhibited 796 pictures at the Old Water-Colour Society, made thousands of pounds and died in poverty. Varley's work was influenced by Claude, Poussin and Girtin. His book, *A Treatise on Zodiacal Physiognomy*, is a curiosity.

VIADUCT AT CHIRK, NORTH WALES

JOHN VARLEY

Signed and dated 1820.

By permission of the Fine Art Society, Ltd.

[11¼ × 20½ in.]

CORNELIUS VARLEY

1781—1873 ('OLD SOCIETY')

ROGET describes Cornelius Varley at the end of his life as a bright little old man, with white beard, deep-set eye and rapid articulation. There is a photographic portrait that gives this water-colourist and scientist the look of a wizard. Indeed, he was a practical wizard, for he not only solved to a creditable extent the mysteries of art, but won renown as an inventor. John Varley, his brother, taught him to paint. In 1811 he patented the graphic telescope, an instrument whereby portraits and landscapes might be drawn with greater facility, and for this he received belatedly a gold medal at the Great Exhibition of 1851. He was made a member of the Society of Arts in 1814. He was also something of a poet, and wrote an ingenious adaptation of the *Marseillaise*, the opening verse of which is as follows:

SONG TO THE GENEROUS IN ART

Ye sons of Art awake to Glory,
Hark, hark what honours bid you rise,
Your Children, Wives and Grandsires hoary,
Behold their fears and raise their joys;
Shall hateful Dealers mischief breeding
With hireling hosts, a greedy race,
Corrupt and enervate our Taste,
While skill and Poetry lies bleeding?
  To Arts, to Arts ye brave,
  Your generous souls set loose.
Paint on, Paint on, all hearts resolved
On Poetry and Grace.

Cornelius Varley was described by a lady who knew him as a great character. He insisted that his daughters always wore green frocks. The Varley *ménage* in Kentish Town was full of scientific toys, 'electric batteries, microscopes, megaphones, telegraphs and telephones, *camerae obscurae*, a telescope, etc. Music, both on orthodox and eccentric instruments, played its part in the entertainment of their guests'. Cornelius Varley had ten children, and three of his sons were devoted to science, one, Cromwell Varley, becoming very celebrated and associated with the history of the Atlantic cable.

THE MARKET PLACE, ROSS, HEREFORDSHIRE

CORNELIUS VARLEY

Signed and dated 1803.

By permission of the Victoria and Albert Museum.

[11⅝ × 18 in.]

71

WILLIAM HAVELL

1782–1857 ('Old Society')

BORN in Reading, William Havell was one of the fourteen children of the drawing-master at the Reading Grammar School. Several of the Havells were artists; William was famous early in life for his handling of the water-colour method. Not only in his art but in his life he had an adventurous disposition. In 1816 he sailed in the *Alceste* for China as artist to the embassy of Lord Amherst. The occasion was anything but plain sailing. There were quarrels aboard ship, and Lord Amherst, refusing to kowtow to the Emperor of China at Peking, failed to get audience with the celestial majesty. On January 27, 1817, the party embarked at Macao for Manila. Havell, leaving the ship at Macao, transferred to the *Lyra* and eventually found himself in India. Here he set up as a landscape and portrait painter, remaining in the neighbourhood of Calcutta for eight years. Another account, however, states that the *Alceste*, with Havell aboard, was wrecked off the Loochoo Islands, that the artist found his way to India and Burma, and in Burma made a considerable fortune by portrait painting. Certain it is that he had returned to Europe by 1828, for his address in the catalogue of the 'Old Society' for that year is 'Rome'. Havell regarded the scenery round about the Eternal City as inspiring, but Italian food and climate were by no means to his taste. In Rome he insisted upon beefsteaks and mutton chops, and found an Englishwoman who could cook for him 'a complete English dinner, without either tomtits or yellow-hammers'. Uwins, with whom Havell shared a deserted house at the foot of Vesuvius, writes that they paid a rent of four pounds per annum and that living cost them less than thirty shillings a week including the cook and her wages. 'To see him (Havell) paint is like seeing Paganini play the fiddle.' No artist of his time saw more of the world than did Havell, and his exhibited works include views of India, China, Italy, Wales and England. But with all his universal sense of beauty, versatility and industry he was unable to secure his material fortunes. He died a poor man at High Row, Kensington, on December 16, 1857, and was buried at Kensal Green.

WINDERMERE
WILLIAM HAVELL
By permission of the British Museum.
[9¾ × 13⅜ in.]

73

SAMUEL PROUT

1783–1852 ('Old Society')

THERE should be a special corner of the Elysian Fields for artists who, having struggled through their lives against adversity, ill-health, and modest temperaments, achieved fine works and fame none the less. Considering that Samuel Prout was partly invalided through sunstroke in his boyhood, it is surprising that he lived to within one year of the allotted span. Who would think to look at his drawings of old Continental towns—intricate in design and detail, yet freely and most artistically drawn, crowded with gay little figures—that Prout was frequently in pain and incapacitated? There is a determination in these things that wins our regard and sympathy. Prout, however, was lucky in his time—a time when much that was picturesque in Continental urban life and scene remained unaffected by the machine, when one might sit in the highways of Paris, Rome, Bruges, Basle and Nuremberg and get on with one's work without being driven from the scene by the internal combustion engine. Thus we see in Prout's drawings something of the peace, security and *joie de vivre* that were part of that now despised nineteenth century, which kept the Four Horsemen of the Apocalypse in leash for about four generations. Prout is one of those artists who managed to fulfil himself both as creative worker and teacher, to earn his bread, to pay his bills, and to support his wife and family by the exercise of an amiable talent. His work was popular but not very remunerative; he was a simple soul who demanded from life no more than life was prepared to give. He worked for those two kindly and knowledgeable dealers, the Grundy brothers of Liverpool and Manchester, and the correspondence between them and the artist, which Mr F. Gordon Roe edited, and which was published in the *Old Water-Colour Society's Club*, Volume XXIV, is a revelation of the artist's tragic disabilities towards the end of his life, and of the mutual respect between dealer and artist. Prout is one of the 'little masters'. His interests were more antiquarian and archaeological than landscape. He exhibited first at the Royal Academy, then with the Associated Artists in Water-Colour, but when the latter came to grief in 1812 he was attracted to the 'Old Society' and showed regularly there from 1815 to 1851.

THE TEMPLE OF MINERVA

SAMUEL PROUT

Courtesy of Messrs Thomas Agnew & Sons, Ltd.
[$11\frac{1}{2} \times 8\frac{1}{4}$ in.]

75

THOMAS MILES RICHARDSON, Sen.

1784–1848 ('Old Society')

IN NEWCASTLE-UPON-TYNE Richardson is a great name to conjure with, as the saying goes. T.M., senior, is not only Newcastle's most famous artist, but was also the founder of a dynasty of artists of merit. Four of his sons followed their father's career. He was born at Ballast Hills, Newcastle-upon-Tyne, and early showed his skill with the pencil. It was some years before he was able to concentrate entirely upon art, for he was first apprenticed to a cabinet-maker, and worked thus until 1806. He then became master of St Andrew's School, but, his health breaking down, took a sea voyage to London. Walking along the Strand he saw a drawing of Conway Castle by David Cox in a shop window, which reawakened his desire to become an artist. It was not, however, till 1813 that he resigned his mastership at St Andrew's School and devoted himself entirely to painting. Richardson exhibited subjects taken from the northern counties at the Royal Academy and British Institution, and the many drawings of his native city and the neighbourhood were begun about 1816. None of his ventures, however, as an artist appear to have met with the success they deserved. Nothing daunted, he was determined to encourage the arts in every way he could, and with other enthusiasts Richardson inaugurated in 1822 the first Fine Art exhibition in the north of England, the exhibition taking place at his own home in Newcastle; the result was the inception of the Northern Academy of Arts and the North of England Society for the Promotion of the Fine Arts. In 1833 he began in partnership with his brother, Moses Aaron Richardson, to issue mezzotint illustrations of the castles of the English and Scottish borders. This venture failed for lack of subscribers. Richardson combined both the romantic and classical temperaments to a marked degree, and could paint such large pictures as *The Entrance to the Shrine of Henry V, Westminster Abbey*, and *Melrose by Moonlight*, or such small and elegant water-colours as *Ouseburn Viaduct*, reproduced on the opposite page. Here is a drawing composed with great skill and instinct with poetic imagination. It was Newcastle that showed us the way to travel about by steam propulsion. Did Richardson realize, even in those exciting days of early trains, that machines were merely incidental to human progress, and by no means indispensable to human happiness? The delicate viaduct and primitive engines are like a vision on the immemorial landscape, while the ploughman and his team remain realities ever steadfast to natural laws.

OUSEBURN VIADUCT

THOMAS MILES RICHARDSON, SEN.

By permission of the Laing Art Gallery, Newcastle-upon-Tyne.

[10¼ × 16¾ in.]

A. V. COPLEY FIELDING

1787 - 1855 ('Old Society')

WHEN ONE recalls how difficult it is to paint one water-colour moderately well one must marvel at the profitable industry of Copley Fielding who exhibited no less than 1,784 such works at the 'Old Society', of which he was made a member in 1812. We cannot say precisely why this artist fails to be really great. It is not that he painted too many. Turner achieved a far greater number and kept his unassailably supreme place. Perhaps it is Fielding's lack of research into nature and his contentment with similar effects that deprive him of a position among the first masters. He was equally adept at marine, mountain and downland subjects and, according to Ruskin, 'he produced some of the most perfect and faultless passages of mist and rain cloud which art has ever seen'. Though Fielding was not actually a pupil of John Varley's, he was friendly with Varley, to whom he showed some of his early efforts. It would seem from a statement by Cornelius Varley that his brother John was by no means impressed with Fielding's talent at first. After a year under Varley's influence Fielding was considered good enough to become an associate of the 'Old Society', and his life-work henceforth was connected with the Society's famous gallery in Pall Mall East. Fielding had a charm of personality and an administrative ability which were invaluable assets when, in 1832, he became President of the Society, a position he held for twenty-three of the most prosperous years of its career. We learn that the young Queen Victoria visited the exhibition in 1838, and was graciously pleased to approve of it and purchase several pictures. The Society was then moving forward to an era of consistent good fortune, when carriages congested Pall Mall, and rank, fashion and riches competed for the annual exhibits. It was unanimously felt that Fielding was an exceptional President, and when he died on March 3, 1855, the general opinion among the members was that 'much of its prosperity had been due for a great many years to the exertions of their late "friend and president"'. It was agreed to defer for a time the election of a new President, 'as a mark of respect to the memory of him they had lost'.

THE VALE OF NEATH (1854)
A. V. COPLEY FIELDING

By permission of N. J. Harrison, Esq.
[25 × 39 in.]

FRANCIS WHEATLEY

R.A.

1747-1801

ONE OF the most popular series of drawings ever made was Wheatley's *Cries of London*. When first 'hot from the press', they delighted the eighteenth-century public, and are still fascinating 'incidents' of any domestic interior. Wheatley has been accused of idealizing the 'lower orders', but every artist knows that beauty pervades the scene everywhere, and a Billingsgate fisher-girl may yet boast the features of some legendary goddess. It just so happened that Wheatley sought charming figures and faces in the byways of the town and found them 'all-alive-O'. Having been born in Wild Court, Covent Garden, the artist in youth had every opportunity of studying the London type as he went from the Piazza to Shipley's school of art, and later to the Royal Academy Schools in the Strand. Wheatley must have shown extraordinary talent to have entered the Schools so early, and to win awards from the Society of Arts before he was twenty. Being a friend of that phenomenal figure-draughtsman, John Hamilton Mortimer, and assisting him in decorative work, his training in life and art was unusually complete. Maybe Wheatley suffered from facility of expression. He had to keep pace with his own private extravagances and give the market what it wanted. As Mr Gordon Roe writes, 'Wheatley has been branded for an improvident soul', and is said to 'have had a roving eye into the bargain'; his adventures in love, not to mention his two marriages and seven children, were no small incentive to industry when he was in the mood. He was elected A.R.A. in 1790 and R.A. in 1791. Wheatley's landscapes in water-colour are not generally known, but that he had skill in using the transparent medium for the expression of rural scenery is proved by such works as *Donnybrook Fair* in the Victoria and Albert Museum, and *Lakeland Scene* reproduced on the opposite page.

LAKELAND SCENE
FRANCIS WHEATLEY, R.A.

Signed and dated 1798.

By permission of Mrs I. J. Dunne.
[15 × 19 in.]

THOMAS GIRTIN

1775–1802

To SEPARATE rumour from fact would deprive the world of many exciting legends. Whether true or not, the story that young Tom Girtin, of Great Bandy Leg Walk, Southwark, rebelled against his master, Edward Dayes, because of the drudgery imposed on him and was imprisoned in Bridewell, is amusing. It was probably the best thing that Dayes, agent of Destiny, could have done for Girtin, for the angry apprentice employed his enforced leisure by decorating the walls of his cell with drawings. Somebody must have told the Earl of Essex of Girton's plight, and the Earl, recognizing the youth's genius, had him released.[1] From that moment his fame, fortune and future were assured, but the future was to be very brief. Girtin was consumptive, and had only a decade in which to achieve his life-work. During the ten years from 1792 to 1802 Girtin became the first master of water-colour painting, and there are connoisseurs who still regard him as unrivalled. Experimenting with the topographical tradition Girton turned the old formula into a thing of beauty that is a joy for ever. A profound student of nature and atmospheric effect, a draughtsman of supreme sensibility, Girtin's work reveals dignity in whatever the subject—a vista of the Thames, a mountain scene like *Scaw Fell*, an old cottage, a piece of architecture like the *Porte St Denis*. His short life is soon told. Son of a brush-maker, apprenticed to Dayes, protégé of Dr Monro, generous, popular, social, friend of the Earl of Harewood for whom he designed the garden statuary at Harewood, numbering among his pupils a 'store of Ladies', Girtin was the darling of fortune. Turner, of the same age, always had the greatest admiration for Tom Girtin, with whom he worked as a lad at Monro's. A critical connoisseur, telling Turner that he had a finer drawing in his hackney coach than any of Turner's, was silenced with the remark, 'Well, if you have a finer drawing than any of mine, it is Tom Girtin's *Chelsea Reach*.' After the Peace of Amiens in 1801, Girtin visited Paris and made a series of water-colours of the French capital—his swan-song.

[1] This romantic legend was printed by W. Thornbury in his *Life of J. M. W. Turner, R.A.*, and repeated with modifications by J. L. Roget in his *History of the 'Old Water-Colour' Society*. Mr Randall Davies, in *Thomas Girtin's Water-Colours* (1924), threw doubt upon it. Certainly, he discovered that nobody of the name of Girtin appears in the Bridewell records for the essential period.

ROMANTIC LANDSCAPE

THOMAS GIRTIN

By permission of Mrs I. J. Dunne.

[12½ × 19 in.]

J. M. W. TURNER

R.A.

1775–1851

THE GREATEST dramatist, the most imaginative poet, could not invent a character more stupendous than J. M. W. Turner. Son of a barber in Maiden Lane, London, young Turner learned to wield the shaving-brush as well as the paint brush. An infant prodigy, he curled perukes while he tried to improve on the sublimities of nature. Drawings done between the ages of seventeen and twenty are already mature. At twenty-four he is an A.R.A., and a full member at twenty-eight. Turner is Professor of Perspective at thirty-three, lecturing to the learned in not too lucid a language. Noble patrons and dealers competed for his work, and his exhibits at the Royal Academy were nearly always the pictures of the year. Though in the glare of publicity, he tried to live in obscurity, with several domiciles, keeping his movements secret from his brother-academicians. Turner travelled about like a topographical tramp, spending little on his own comfort. Most of the beauty-spots in Britain, France and Italy were known to him, and no artist has left so varied a collection of subjects and methods of treating them. Turner's *Liber Studiorum*, in itself, would be enough to establish the fame of any artist, but he did thousands upon thousands of sketches, finished drawings and paintings. Praised and patronized in his youth, Turner was abused unmercifully by the critics for his later impressionistic works, until Ruskin, young, enthusiastic, idolatrous, defended him in his monumental work *Modern Painters*. The artist was then past caring who praised or blamed. Though he had amassed a huge fortune he lived in self-inflicted poverty—a recluse. Under the name of Booth, the name of his housekeeper, he took lodgings in Cheyne Walk, Chelsea, the better to study river and sky effects continually; and here, old, ailing, aware of his greatness, but also aware that he had not entirely realized his dreams, he died looking at the sun, tended devotedly by Mrs Booth. Turner was buried in the crypt of St Paul's cathedral on December 30, 1851. From a confused will it was discovered that the artist had left £140,000 to establish an asylum for distressed artists. Pictures and drawings in Turner's possession at his death were left to the nation. The will was contested, and a chancery suit lasted for some years. Much of his funded property was successfully claimed by the next of kin, £20,000 went to the Royal Academy, and a hundred oil paintings and about 19,000 drawings were allotted to the State.

FORUM ROMANUM
J. M. W. TURNER, R.A.

Formerly in Mr F. J. Nettlefold's Collection, and presented by him to the
National Gallery of Canada, Ottawa.

[$5\frac{1}{2} \times 8\frac{1}{2}$ in.]

JOHN SELL COTMAN

1782–1842 ('OLD SOCIETY')

ASTERPIECES are inseparably linked with the name of Christie. At the great auction rooms the drama of art and money plays on, generation after generation. *Sunt lachrymae rerum.* There could have been no more pathetic sale than that of John Sell Cotman's 'lots' in 1836. Imagine a tall, grey-haired man of fifty-four, looking older than his years, standing anxiously among dealers and collectors waiting for the auction to begin. It is John Sell Cotman, one of the world's greatest water-colourists. His genius is about to be weighed in the balance against gold. Experience could have taught him that the world thought little of his efforts, for he had known 'penury and despair', and was able to live only by reason of a modestly paid art-mastership at King's College. But hope dies harder in the heart of an artist than with ordinary mortals. The auctioneer is now handling a little drawing called *Greta Bridge*. What offers? Not even a guinea! It is so cheap in the eyes of the connoisseurs that shillings will suffice. 'Any advance on eight shillings?' There is silence until the hammer falls. Knocked down for eight shillings! Somebody, who doesn't know it, has possessed himself of a masterpiece which will allure, excite and inspire the lovers of art for all time. 'My *Greta Bridge*,' sighed Cotman. 'Ah, I was happy when I painted that, young, ambitious, hopeful of success.' Since the *Greta* had failed, what chance have the others? The auctioneer is showing Cotman's *Dismasted Brig*, a derelict in a trough of the waves, menaced by storm clouds closing in upon it. 'How much for the old ship?' Shillings again. Seventeen shillings. 'Any advance on seventeen?' The hammer falls. 'Seventeen shillings—to Mr Cotman.' The artist had bought it back. But the name of John Sell Cotman has come through all the storms of mortality and is beyond the avarice of time. *Greta Bridge* and *Dismantled Brig* are now among the treasures of the British Museum, and wherever water-colourists foregather John Sell Cotman, though dead over a hundred years, is a presiding and honoured guest. A leading member of our great Norwich school of landscape painting, he practised his art and taught in Norwich, studied in London, met Girtin and Varley, and was patronized by Dawson Turner. In 1834 he returned to London and took up a position as drawing-master at King's College. Cotman died in 1842 and was buried in the grounds of St John's Wood Chapel. *Cader Idris from Barmouth Sands* is also one of Cotman's masterpieces.

CADER IDRIS FROM BARMOUTH SANDS

JOHN SELL COTMAN

Formerly in Mr F. J. Nettlefold's Collection, and presented by him to the Diploma
Gallery of the Royal Society of Painters in Water-Colours.

[14¾ × 21½ in.]

DAVID COX

1783–1859 ('Old Society')

ON September 22, 1856, 'Farmer' Cox, as Turner called him, signed his name for the last time in the visitors' book at the Royal Oak, Bettws-y-coed, 'and never, except in his mind's eye, saw his dear Bettws again'. This place was his chief inspiration. He died on June 7, 1859. Perhaps the most lovable, and certainly one of the best, interpreters of the English scene, departed this life with a 'God bless you' to his sorrowing relatives and friends, and a 'farewell, pictures, I shall never see you again'. As he died, so he had lived, devout, humble, affectionate, always with some dream of beauty in his mind and heart. The son of a blacksmith, Cox was none the less the born aristocrat, seeking perfection in all things, and frequently attaining it in his work. Until nearing the end of his life he had spent much of his time in teaching, time that he would have preferred to give to creative work. He could, however, look back on a happy and well regulated life, and if his material rewards were not large his spiritual gains were incalculable. There is a divinity that shapes our ends, and Cox's fate was decided when, as a boy, he fell over a doorscraper and injured his leg. This rendered him unfit for the heavy work of a smith, and when some guardian angel placed in the boy's hands a box of paints he set foot on the road to immortality. He is among the great masters of atmospheric effect. His windy, rainy skies are the essence of truth, and his little figures going about their daily tasks are drawn with rare human sympathy. The master's humility and modesty, his anxiety lest he should overcharge for his pictures, is enchanting. His life is best told in Mr F. Gordon Roe's book *David Cox, the Master,* but an earlier lover of his work wrote this valedictory notice in *Punch* for May 1859, addressing the painter. 'I feel as if you and I were shaking hands for a long, long parting. Is it the wavy mist of tears in my eyes, or the dimness of years in yours, that blears those Welsh mountains and wild western moorlands, the last, I fear, from your glorious old hand—true to the heart as ever, but now trembling—will create for the pleasure of all that have ever looked nature lovingly in the face? . . . Go, my dear young friends, reverently and tenderly, and give your farewell and God-speed to old David Cox, for he will draw no more.'

WORCESTERSHIRE LANDSCAPE
David Cox

By permission of Mrs I. J. Dunne.
[18 × 25 in.]

PETER DE WINT

1784–1849 ('Old Society')

IF BY 'virtue' of scientific materialism England is planned out of existence, the moon is populated, or the universe charted for super-jets, a lover of old-fashioned things might still be able to see in Peter de Wint's works the kind of earthly paradise that has always existed for those who have eyes to see and hearts to feel. A god-fearing man, who read the Bible every day, and thanked heaven for the gift of water-colour painting, de Wint was privileged to record his impressions of the beauties of nature with lyrical and passionate joy. His works are like psalms in water-colour, songs of praise for the gift of trees, pastures, hills, lakes, rivers, bridges, cathedrals and cottages. The cattle that come down to drink at the stream in the cool of a summer evening might have been created specially for his infallible brush. At harvest-time he was with the harvesters and gleaners, adding his quota of labour and gratitude for the fruits of the earth. Such mellow serenity haunts his work that a Peter de Wint must remind us of the places and people we most loved and where and when we were happiest. One of the great constellation of artists that rose towards the end of the eighteenth century, de Wint became a master of the English rustic scene. His life was like one of those placid streams, bordered with trees, scintillating with light, so typical of his work. Born at Stone in Staffordshire, of Dutch ancestry, de Wint was one of Dr Monro's protégés, studied at the Royal Academy Schools, married Harriet Hilton, sister of William Hilton, R.A., his life-long friend—an ideally happy marriage. Harriet could write to Peter after forty years of marriage, 'Nothing can compensate for the pain of being parted', when he was on one of his sketching expeditions. An early member of the 'Old Society', de Wint did moderately well, had many pupils and kept a good house in Gower Street. He died in 1849. A little marble cross marks his resting place in the Chapel of the Savoy. *The Valley of the Thames and Cliveden Woods* and a few other drawings by de Wint, hung in the right room, would give the idea of a perpetual summer.

THE VALLEY OF THE THAMES AND CLIVEDEN WOODS
Peter de Wint

By permission of T. W. Bacon, Esq.
[$11\frac{3}{4} \times 18\frac{3}{8}$ in.]

SIR DAVID WILKIE

R.A.

1785–1841

DAVID WILKIE was one of the infant prodigies of art. Even among the Italian masters there could have been few who could draw with such facility at so early an age. His biographers tell us that he could draw before he could read or even talk distinctly. With such intuitive genius it is not surprising that his picture *Village Politicians*, painted before he was twenty-one, achieved renown at the Royal Academy of 1806, and that thenceforward Wilkie went on from success to success, winning the patronage of the Prince Regent and the Duke of Wellington among other famous men. His subjects, full of lively character somewhat after the Dutch manner, *The Penny Wedding*, *Blind Man's Buff*, *Reading of a Will*, were immensely popular. His most famous picture is *Chelsea Pensioners listening to the News of Waterloo*. The canny Scots relative who warned David that 'daubin' wi' a stick' would not bring him any money would have been staggered could he have seen the Duke of Wellington pay Wilkie a thousand guineas in banknotes for this picture, as his Grace preferred to do rather than give Wilkie a draft on his bankers, saying that he did not wish them to know that he had been such a d—d fool as to pay so much for a picture. It is possible that Wilkie was tired of the monotony of success, and so, poor in health and dispirited by the death of his mother, wandered abroad in 1824. His contact with the old Continental masters completely revolutionized his style and not for the better. He abandoned his essential gift for living character, and became involved in a manner unsuited to his temperament. His water-colours are very little known but this example is an amazing production, combining detail, breadth and a knowledge of figure drawing wholly indicative of Wilkie's best powers. Few artists could attempt, even fewer succeed, in such a subject, using the water-colour method. Wilkie returned to the East in 1840. While on his way home from Jerusalem he was taken suddenly ill and died on June 1, 1841, and was buried at sea off Gibraltar. An oil version of *Village Festival*, formerly in the Angerstein Collection, is in the National Gallery.

VILLAGE FESTIVAL
Sir David Wilkie, R.A.

By permission of A. Egerton Cooper, Esq., R.B.A., A.R.C.A.

[11½ × 15⅝ in.]

93

RICHARD PARKES BONINGTON

1802–28

IN HIS book *English Water-Colours* Laurence Binyon tells us that Bonington 'was in a fever to reach Venice', and indeed he arrived only just in time, in the spring of 1826. To use Coleridge's remark in regard to Keats, 'there was death in that hand'; for within two years Bonington was to lay aside his brilliant pencil and die. There is some analogy in the lives and works of these two men. Both were lyrical poets of the first magnitude, one in words, the other in paint. Both were supreme 'colourists'. Son of the governor of Nottingham County Jail, Bonington early showed a passion for art, and was helped by his father, who resigned his position at Nottingham and became an artist. Fortune took the Bonington family to France, and there young Richard fell in with that fine water-colourist, Louis Francia, and later that magnificent oil-painter, Delacroix, finally entering the studio of Baron Gros in Paris. As the Napoleonic phase subsided and the Neo-classics, exemplified in David, passed out of fashion, Bonington's rich naturalistic land and seascapes, architectural scenes and illustrations from history found favour. Bonington's French coast views, for their combination of technical power and poetic feeling, have a place to themselves in the pantheon of art. He was equally adept in big oil-paintings and tiny water-colours, such as the *Doge's Palace, Venice*, 45 by 64 inches, and *Sunset*, no larger than $5\frac{1}{2}$ by $7\frac{1}{2}$ inches. It is the sunlight in Bonington's works that is so appealing and influential on his followers. He was a supreme master of effect. A little piece of paper with Bonington's rich and lucid washes would appear to contain a whole world of experience and satisfied longing. Bonington did much to popularize the English art of water-colour in France. As Binyon says, his 'handsome presence, quiet manners, and precocious mastery of the brush' delighted the French artists and critics. More than delighted, for at least one young Frenchman, seeing a Bonington water-colour in a shop window, was moved to become a painter himself. He had been an assistant in a Paris drapery establishment. The young man was Jean Baptiste Camille Corot.

SUNSET IN THE PAYS DE CAUX

RICHARD PARKES BONINGTON

From the original in the Wallace Collection, by permission.

[7½ × 10½ in.]

95

WILLIAM TURNER
(OF OXFORD)
1789–1862 ('OLD SOCIETY')

OF THE several young men who helped to found the fame of the 'Old Society', William Turner (of Oxford) takes pride of place for brilliant work in his youth. In fact I know of no other drawing comparable, as an early and complete work, with this artist's *View in Wychwood Forest*. Since it was exhibited at the 'Old Society' in 1809, it must have been done before Turner was twenty. Need we wonder, therefore, that John Varley, his master, 'spoke violently of a young man who had been his pupil learning to draw in water-colours'. According to Farington, 'Reinagle said, He had never seen drawings to equal them.' Though the *View in Wychwood Forest* shows Varley's admirable teaching it is infused with a poetic grandeur of design and intensity of feeling which proclaim an individual master of the first magnitude. It could hang side by side with any landscape of any period and not lose its authority. May we say that William Turner, a mere youth, had arrived on eagle wing long before other artists, even artists of genius, were fully fledged? How then account for the fact that, though he did much admirable work over a long period of time, he never improved on this drawing or even equalled it? It was probably owing to a certain diffidence, and a contentment with his lot and the lovely Oxford environment in which he chose to live. He had a number of pupils whom he taught in a careful, painstaking manner, but I cannot recall any who made a name in art, except Sir Thomas Jackson, R.A. Something of a 'don' of water-colour painting, William Turner must also have been endowed with no little of the Scholar Gipsy's temperament. While his master, John Varley, was the London celebrity, restless, energetic, inventive, 'violent', to use Farington's expression, while the other Turner was always the centre of controversy, trying to prove that he was as great as if not greater than any other artist, living or dead, William wandered peacefully about Woodstock, Iffley, the Hinkseys and all the places later immortalized by Matthew Arnold in his two poems. For a change of scene the Oxford Turner leaves Bagley Wood and the banks of the Cherwell for other English counties, for Wales and Scotland, but unlike the Scholar Gipsy of the poem he is always returning to Oxford and his friends there. He died on August 7, 1862, and rests in the churchyard of Shipton-on-Cherwell, not far from Blackbourton where he was born.

VIEW IN WYCHWOOD FOREST
WILLIAM TURNER (of Oxford)

Signed W. Turner (Shipston on Cher) Oxon. Exhibited at the Society of
Painters in Water-Colours, 1809.

By permission of the Victoria and Albert Museum.
[23⅞ × 31¼ in.]

WILLIAM HENRY HUNT

1790–1864 ('Old Society')

'As he was fit for nothing they made an artist of him.' Such was the comment by William Henry Hunt's uncle, a butcher. 'Birdsnest Hunt', as he has been affectionately called, is among the admirable artists and characters of his time. Son of a tinplate worker, and born in Bolton (now Endell) Street, London, Hunt impressed his frail personality on the art of water-colour, and won the highest praise from Ruskin. Indeed, the Victorian oracle regarded him as a supreme master. There is not the slightest doubt that the artist can claim to be one of the little masters. His studies of fruit, flowers and birds' nests are unique for high finish and rich, luxuriant colour. He was also equally effective in small figure-compositions of rustic and urban characters with some sentimental or humorous idea, such as the two famous water-colours in the Nettlefold Collection, *The Attack* and *The Defeat*, showing the effect of a large apple pie on a greedy boy. What Hunt lacked in nobility of vision and intellectual inventiveness he made up in the loving care he lavished upon his simple, unaffected themes. The artist developed a style of his own, abandoning the simple direct washes of the Old Masters of water-colour painting for elaborate stipple, frequently on a basis of Chinese white. Asked advice as to how to paint he could not be more lucid than to say 'fudge it out', but this homely expression does actually convey Hunt's methods. His detailed water-colours are, in fact, 'fudged out' by the tireless application of small paint-brushes, touch upon touch until in the fulness of time the fruit, the flower, the grape, the bird's egg takes on an almost incredible simulacrum of reality. Hunt had found a way of painting still life in water-colours with as much finish as earlier masters had painted it in oils, and his efforts were rewarded by popular and critical acclaim. His subjects and style were directly due to the artist's physical deformity. A delicate child, he suffered from a weakness in the legs which made it difficult for him to get about, and for that reason he chose themes which could be painted in the studio. He was a pupil of John Varley and a friend of John Linnell. Much respected by all who knew him, he died on February 10, 1864, and was buried in Highgate Cemetery.

SLUMBER

WILLIAM HENRY HUNT

By permission of the City Museum and Art Gallery, Birmingham.
$[13\frac{5}{8} \times 16\frac{7}{8}$ in.$]$

99

W. CLARKSON STANFIELD

R.A.

1793–1867

SON OF an eminent Irish literary man, Stanfield was born in Sunderland, and like George Chambers and Nicholas Pocock was a professional sailor before he became an artist. His gift for painting manifested itself early when he did the scenery for amateur theatricals. Captain Marryat, the novelist, encouraged him, and when he was discharged from the Navy as the result of an accident he took seriously to art. For a time he worked as scene-painter at the old Royal Theatre, Well-close Square, London, and was afterwards engaged at the Drury Lane, His Majesty's, and Coburg Theatres. With his great friend David Roberts, Stanfield was one of the best scene-painters of his time. He exhibited at the Society of Artists in 1824. Travelling on the Continent, he gathered a mass of material which formed the basis of a large number of easel pictures, particularly views of Italy. Exhibiting at the Royal Academy in 1829, his pictures were so popular that he was made an Associate in 1832 and a full R.A. three years later. William IV commissioned him to paint pictures of Portsmouth Harbour and the opening of the new Waterloo Bridge. Stanfield was friendly with the great Turner, and there was not a little genial professional rivalry between them. An amusing story is told by Thornbury in his *Life of Turner*. He writes: 'In 1826 that great ruler of the sea, Stanfield, painted a picture of a calm which he named *Throwing the Painter* (rope). Unfortunately he was unable to get it finished in time for the Exhibition, and Calcott (*sic*) hearing of it, painted a picture which for fun he called *Dutch Fishing Boats missing the Painter*. Turner would have a rare chuckle over these studio jokes, and quietly determining to cap them all, he came out next year with a work named *Now for the Painter* with all the laughing triumph of a boy who at leap-frog takes the last and highest back.' This great picture was presented by Mr F. J. Nettlefold in 1947 to the Manchester City Art Gallery. Stanfield accompanied Turner to the farewell lunch given to Dickens at Greenwich immediately before the novelist's trip to Italy in 1842.

ST MICHAEL'S MOUNT
W. CLARKSON STANFIELD, R.A.

By permission of Mrs I. J. Dunne.
[8¾ × 13¼ in.]

DAVID ROBERTS

R.A.

1796–1864

THE SPIRIT OF TIME, contemplating the scene at Christie's in May 1865, when over a thousand 'lots' of David Roberts's work were being dispersed for the sum of about seventeen thousand pounds, might have murmured 'Well done, Davie!' For here was a life that had shone with brilliance out of a dark and unpromising origin. What intimations of immortality, what divine spark had urged this son of a poor Edinburgh cobbler to rise above environment and heredity and become so distinguished and successful an artist? As the father wore the night hours down repairing the soles of Auld Reekie, David knelt on the top of an old chest drawing as if his life depended upon it. The obvious job for one so skilful with the brush was a house-painter's, so Roberts junior was apprenticed and began earning the living of two shillings a week, from five in the morning, with an increase of sixpence a year. Whatever spare time he had was spent in sketching. After seven years of house-decorating, Destiny found him work as scene-painter, touring the north of England with a theatrical company, and looking with adoring eyes at great church architecture, particularly York Minster. David Roberts has written, 'Here, I may say, I first became a painter. . . . Is there a part of that old Minster I do not know? . . .' In 1822 Roberts was appointed scene-painter to Drury Lane Theatre. Domiciled in London, the artist, with his friends Clarkson Stanfield, George Chambers, J. M. Wright and John Wilson, was responsible for all the scene-painting of importance, and until the age of thirty-two he was engaged on this work. Thereafter he devoted himself to fine art, and became a member of various societies, including the Royal Academy. He was now free to travel about Europe. The sumptuous architecture of Burgos, Toledo, Cordova, Seville and Granada inspired him with innumerable drawings and paintings during the eighteen-thirties. Later he toured Egypt and the Holy Land, Belgium, France, Holland and Italy. His pictures were so popular with collectors that an enterprising publisher, F. G. Moon, published a book of them in parts during 1842 and 1849 entitled *Views in the Holy Land, Syria, Idumea, Arabia, Egypt and Nubia,* with 250 plates in chromo-lithography, the whole work costing no less than £50,000 to produce.

THE BRIDGE AT TOLEDO
DAVID ROBERTS, R.A.

By permission of Mrs I. J. Dunne.
[12¼ × 20½ in.]

103

WILLIAM EVANS
(OF ETON)
1798–1877 ('Old Society')

WILLIAM EVANS is unique among water-colourists in that there is a house at Eton named after him. Evans's House has been known to generations of Etonians. It was founded and run by Evans, who succeeded his father as drawing-master at the famous college in 1823. He was intended for the medical profession but, his father's health failing, he developed a natural taste for drawing and was able to take on the work at Eton. His daughter, Mrs W. M. Fenn, wrote that 'though quite unprepared for the work, he went into the Drawing School so persistently and diligently that in a very few years he was master of his position. "At first", he said, "the older boys knew more of drawing than he did", but this did not discourage him, and allowing himself only four hours' sleep he devoted his whole time to art.' This paragraph reveals Evans's will-power and determination; and from all accounts he was a strong and benevolent personality, very tall and powerfully built and as much interested in sport as in art. He was a member of that rare society called Psychrolutes. The rule was that one had to bathe *al fresco* daily from November to March. The leader and professors were renowned for skill in swimming and diving, and the season concluded with a presidential address on the river bank 'to which Psychrolutes listened in dripping state before the application of the towel was permitted'. With its spirit of eternal youth against a background of venerable buildings, the Thames, and the Castle across the playing-fields, Eton gave Evans all that he desired. While he presided over Evans's House, he himself lived in the Cottage in Keate's Lane for fifty years and died there on December 31, 1877. His best work was inspired by the traditional festivals and games at Eton: *Procession of Boats, The Cricket Field, The Wall Game* and *Ad Montem;* but Evans varied these jubilant themes with drawings of Scotland and the Riviera. His art was influenced by Peter de Wint, from whom he took a few lessons. It is an interesting fact that four generations of the Evans family were art masters at Eton, the last of them being Mr W. Sydney V. Evans, who retired just before 1939.

THE CRICKET FIELD, ETON
WILLIAM EVANS (of Eton)

By permission of Miss N. O. Radcliffe-Platt.
[26¾ × 37 in.]

JAMES HOLLAND

1799–1870 ('Old Society')

O F THE many artists who have painted Venice, James Holland is among the best. If he has not the imagination of J. M. W. Turner or the distinction of Bonington, Holland has vigour of presentation and that riotous colour which is inseparable from the magical *Bride of the Sea*. It was perhaps a fortunate chance that made Holland begin as a flower-painter, if only on pottery, for his studies of flowers for this utilitarian purpose were to develop a colour-sense invaluable to the artist when he came face to face with the turquoise and rose, the solemn green and antique gold mysteries of Venetian lagoon, palace, bridge and *calle*. Although Holland painted elsewhere on the Continent it is his Venetian mood that comes to mind in thinking of his work. The *Rialto Bridge*, in the Victoria and Albert Museum, *The Gondola, Venice*, and *Venice*, lately in the Nettlefold Collection, are replete with architectural knowledge and poetic sentiment. Ruskin is curiously inconsistent in his remarks about Holland's work. In Section V. of *Modern Painters* ('Of Truth of Water', Chapter 11), he writes: 'Of Water as painted by the moderns I have seen, some seven years ago, works by J. Holland which were, I think, as near perfection as truth of water can be carried—for *bona fide* truth, refined and finished to the highest degree. But he has since that time produced worse pictures every year, and his fate appears irrecoverable, unless by a very strong effort and total change of system.' In the final edition of his work, however, Ruskin has deleted the whole passage. The fact is that Holland, though beginning his career at a moment when the water-colour school had lost its first youth and was becoming a matter of virtuosity rather than inspiration, retained to a creditable degree the fine delineation and limpid wash of the earlier masters. Holland was born at Burslem, and Colonel M. H. Grant, in that indispensable work of his, *Chronological History of the Old English Landscape Painters*, informs us that 'his grandfather was Thomas Holland of Burslem, described in a Survey of 1786 as "Manufacturer of Black and Red China Ware and Gilder".' There would appear to be some mystery as to Holland's paternity, for Mr R. G. Haggar discovered an entry in the Burslem registers under baptisms for 1805, as follows: December 25th, James Holland, son of Martha Holland, illegit., October 18th, 1799.[1]

[1] See *Apollo*, August 1948.

THE DOGE'S PALACE, VENICE

JAMES HOLLAND

Courtesy of Messrs Thomas Agnew & Sons, Ltd.

[13½ × 19½ in.]

107

FREDERICK TAYLER

1802–89 ('Old Society')

THE SON of a country gentleman, with an estate at Boreham Wood, Elstree, Herts, Frederick Tayler was educated at both Eton and Harrow with a view to taking up holy orders. Owing to the financial failure of his father, however, Tayler was thrown much upon his own resources, and decided to take up the career of art. He began to study at Sass's School, and continued at the Royal Academy. Thence, he went to Horace Vernet's studio in Paris. Perhaps his greatest influence was R. P. Bonington whom Tayler met in Paris. No doubt Bonington's brilliant water-colour work inspired Tayler to become proficient in this method rather than to continue painting in oils. His own early love of sport directed his talents towards animal subjects, and he soon became famous for his pictures of horses, dogs, and stags. Tayler was never happier than when working in the Scottish Highlands, and many of his best pictures are scenes in the far north. The artist was also interested in period costume and composed many stag-hunts and hawking-parties in eighteenth-century dress. Tayler graduated from the associateship of the 'Old Society' in 1831 to President in 1858, a position that he held for thirteen years. Ruskin greatly admired his powerful *sketching*, as he called it. 'Few drawings of the present day', he writes, in the first volume of *Modern Painters*, 'involve greater sensations of power. Every dash tells, and the quantity of effect obtained is enormous, in proportion to the apparent means.' The Victorian oracle, however, regarded Tayler's work as merely *sketching*. He may even have considered the water-colour reproduced on the opposite page as a sketch, so insistent at times was Ruskin on high finish, but to us this study of a huntsman and hounds is full of relevant detail. Few water-colourists today carry their work so far. Tayler died in 1889, and was buried in Hampstead Cemetery.

HUNTSMAN AND HOUNDS
FREDERICK TAYLER

Signed with monogram, and dated 1865.

By permission of Mrs I. J. Dunne.
[14 × 20 in.]

EDWARD DUNCAN

1803–82 ('Old Society')

WRITING about Edward Duncan, Randall Davies aptly suggested that the great forerunners of water-colour painting laid the foundation of their art so well and truly that the Victorian follower had little to do but to exploit his talents and come into the harvest of success made more abundant by the great wealth of that era. This is true not only of Duncan but of quite a number of his contemporaries who acquired a facility in depicting landscapes, marine and figure subjects. Duncan, like Copley Fielding, knew as well as anybody the ingredients of picture-making, and year by year achieved a steady flow of saleable work. It is a current affectation to make fun of the so-called representational art of middle Victorian times, but the fact remains that such artists as Duncan thoroughly knew their craft, and some artists with inflated reputations today would be completely lost if they attempted the subjects that Duncan could do with such apparent legerdemain. Apprenticed when very young to Robert Havell, the aquatint engraver, he was well grounded in technique, and worked on sporting subjects for Fores, the dealer, in Piccadilly. He exhibited at the British Institution, joined the New Society of Water-Colour Painters in 1834 and eventually became a member of the 'Old Society', where he continued throughout a long life to exhibit. Such drawings as *Spithead* in the City Art Gallery, Birmingham, and *Whitby* in the Victoria and Albert Museum have charm of colour and an expert knowledge of ships. He could draw the figure with equal skill, especially peasants and fisher-folk. Judging by the prices fetched by his works when put up for auction a year or two after his death, he must have made a large income. Duncan, who appears to have been as happy in his social relations as he was in his art, was much respected by his colleagues. Jenkins, Secretary of the 'Old Society' in 1882, wrote: 'Mr Duncan in himself eminently represented one of the finest types of English character. Blest with great talents, a happy disposition, and a vigorous constitution, he worked hard because he loved his work and its art for its own sake. Scrupulously upright, genial, hospitable, very generous, he drew around him an attached circle of devoted friends who have rarely had to deplore the loss of a more estimable or valued life.'

WHITBY

EDWARD DUNCAN

Signed and dated 1841.

Formerly in Mr F. J. Nettlefold's Collection, and presented by him to the
Victoria and Albert Museum.

[15¾ × 23 in.]

III

GEORGE CHAMBERS

1803–40 ('Old Society')

BORN IN a Whitby slum, son of a common seaman, George Chambers would appear to have been 'actuated from birth by the divine principle of genius'. Yet no artist known to fame could have suffered such adversities in youth. Chambers began to work at the age of eight, under-sized and weak in physique, filling sacks with coal. At ten he went to sea. So small was he and so small was his first ship, that he slept in one of the captain's seaboots. But from his earliest years he excited wonder by his skill as painter, decorator and draughtsman of ships. He determined against all odds to excel as a marine artist, and as his work progressed he received commissions from sea-captains and owners. Within a few years he was able to quit his calling as a seaman and devote himself to art. Chambers spent some of his time scene-painting for the theatre. He also assisted in painting the view of London in Mr Horner's Regent's Park Colosseum. His sea-pieces began to attract the naval-officer-collector. Admiral Capell, seeing two of Chambers's marines in a shop in Greek Street, London, enquired about the artist and became his friend. The erstwhile cabin-boy had come as it were out of the ship's galley on to the bridge. Everybody, whatever his class, liked and admired young Chambers as much for his genius as for his modest demeanour. Lord Mark Kerr intro-duced the artist to the King, and William IV received him with sailor-like camaraderie. John Watkins, Chambers's first biographer, tells this delightful story of their meeting at Windsor. 'Well, Mr Chambers,' said the King, 'howdy'e do? I've been expecting you. Let me see what you have brought.' Chambers opened his portfolio of sketches and turned them over for the King's view. 'Ah, very good, very good,' said William. 'I'll go and bring Adelaide —there is a good light here.' With that he walked away and presently returned, leading the Queen, arm in arm. 'This is Mr Chambers,' he said, 'he has brought his sketches for you to look at—I would like to see your choice.' Taking up a sketch of a storm scene, he said, 'I would choose that.' The Queen replied, 'I don't like that,—it is too terrible.' 'Oh, Ma'am,' he said with a smile, 'we sailors like such subjects best—eh, Mr Chambers?' However, the Queen chose a view of Dover and another of Greenwich. . . . Chambers enjoyed his fame as Marine Painter Royal for about five years. His health weakened by early hardship, he died at the age of thirty-seven, having achieved a foremost place among marine painters.

HAYBOATS ON THE MEDWAY

GEORGE CHAMBERS

Signed and dated 1837.

By permission of the City Museum and Art Gallery, Birmingham.

[11¼ × 15¼ in.]

SAMUEL PALMER

1805–81 ('OLD SOCIETY')

IN HIS life of his father, A. H. Palmer gives us a charming description of the young Samuel Palmer walking from Soho to Linnell's house at Hampstead with old William Blake. As they approached the house a merry troop of children rushed forth to meet them, and once they were inside Mrs Linnell made them welcome. There were jolly feasts, much talk of art, and many a song sung at the piano by Mrs Linnell after the board had been cleared. On those walks to and fro Palmer received inspiration from William Blake. The young man profited by the visionary's beautiful mind; and it might be said that his own became impregnated with Blake's dreams, and was able to carry them forward with greater versatility and lucidity than the master. Samuel Palmer is one of the most poetic interpreters of landscape. Looking at his work, especially his earlier drawings, he seems to have inherited that changeless, timeless pastoral mood of all the poets from Theocritus to Gray. His drawings veritably 'sing'. His soul was steeped in the joys and melancholies of the country muse. He is all Milton's *Allegro* and *Penseroso*. He lived with the great poets, and indeed translated and illustrated Virgil's *Eclogues*. To say that Palmer was in advance of his time in that his work was free, vigorous, original and sometimes brilliantly coloured, means really nothing. Rather we would say that Palmer, like all great landscapists, had the eternal sense, and a vision and technique equal to his love of nature. If such a drawing as *In a Shoreham Garden* goes beyond nature and strains credulity it only emphasizes the intense feeling of the artist; and there are others in the same category: *The Magic Apple Tree*, *The Timber Wagon*, *The Golden Valley* and *The Orange Twilight*. They have the grandeur of genius; they are not the result of eccentricity, but improvisations on the profound meditative experience to be seen in such masterpieces as the *City of Rome* and *The Vatican*. Palmer came from a family of clergymen, and as a boy was deeply read in the Bible and English and Latin literature. He first exhibited at the age of fourteen. As Mr Martin Hardie says, his work 'has a largeness and permanence, as though he were picturing not one evening, but all evenings; not one village, but all the ample comfort and beauty of our English countryside; not one homeward journey after the day's toil, but the whole pilgrimage of life.' *Hailsham—Sussex. Storm Coming On* was done when Palmer was only sixteen.

HAILSHAM—SUSSEX.   STORM COMING ON
Samuel Palmer

By permission of Leonard Duke, Esq.
[8 5/16 × 12 1/2 in.]

CHARLES BENTLEY

1806–54 ('OLD SOCIETY')

ONE OF the reasons why our water-colourists were so distinguished is because their training began early and continued until they had mastered their materials and tools. They were, for the most part, apprentices, and learned their 'trade' thoroughly. The system produced far better results than those of the modern art school. Charles Bentley, son of an artisan, having shown talent for drawing, was placed with one of the Fielding brothers, Theodore Henry Adolphus, to learn aquatinting. That such apprentices had to work long hours is proved by the fact that William Callow, fellow-pupil and friend of Bentley's at the same studio, worked from 8 a.m. to 6 p.m. daily. In his capacity as apprentice Bentley went to Paris, and may have assisted in the production of the *Excursion sur les Côtes et dans les Ports de Normandie* (Paris, 1823–5). Most of the plates for that book being after drawings by Bonington, it is more than likely that the latter directed Bentley's taste towards marine painting. Bentley's articles expiring in 1827, he was employed in designing plates for various periodicals which were then becoming popular. He exhibited at the New Society (now Royal Institute) of Painters in Water-Colours in 1832 and 1833, but in 1834 he became an Associate-Exhibitor of the 'Old Society'. He is best known for his seascapes. During the artist's lifetime, however, his success was never equal to his merits. He was highly praised by the critics, and obituary articles in the *Athenaeum* and the *Art Journal* leave us in no doubt as to the contemporary attitude of informed opinion; but as Samuel Redgrave remarked, Bentley 'was uncertain in his transactions and always poor'. When he was not travelling the coasts in search of subjects, the artist's life was confined to the neighbourhood of Tottenham Court Road where he was born. He lived variously at Bateman's Buildings, Mornington Place and Charlotte Street, London's original 'Latin Quarter' a hundred years ago. Bentley died of cholera on September 4, 1854.

DUNLUCE CASTLE, COUNTY ANTRIM, IRELAND

CHARLES BENTLEY

By permission of the Victoria and Albert Museum.
[21½ × 32 in.]

WILLIAM CALLOW

1812–1908 ('Old Society')

ONE DOES not need to be old to remember the stately form of William Callow entering Mr Augustus Walker's gallery in Bond Street. To see Callow was to meet a man who had been associated with most of the great artists of the nineteenth century. Here was somebody who had spoken with Turner, Cox, Constable and de Wint—a matter for veneration in itself; but as Martin Hardie writes, 'The atmosphere of the Royal Society of Painters in Water-Colours must contain some benign and salubrious element which conduces to longevity'. No fewer than fifteen of its members since 1804 reached or passed their ninetieth year. William Callow's life was one of consistent success and serenity. Apprenticed to Theodore Fielding at the age of eleven, he was only seventeen when he went to Paris to assist a Swiss artist named Ostenwald in the production of a book on Switzerland. This was the beginning of those Continental peregrinations which were so important a part of his life and art. France for many years became Callow's second home, and it was in Paris that he met Thomas Shotter Boys, whose work was to have a profound influence on him. Boys had known Bonington, and the aesthetic genealogy is easily traced. Callow's English and French views, exhibited all over France, were immensely popular, and he numbered among his pupils members of the old French nobility. He taught the Princess Clémentine d'Orléans twice a week for nearly seven years. The artist was a great walker, wandering all over France, Italy, Germany, and Switzerland, and filling innumerable sketch books with delicate pencil drawings, which he used as the basis for elaborate water-colours, relying on his memory for colour effects. With such a fine technical knowledge as he had acquired in his youth from the Fieldings, and with the influence of Boys and Bonington, Callow seldom fails to please us with his views of nature and of the architectural curiosities of old cities in England and on the Continent. In fact, Callow's work, as a whole, is a revelation of the lovely world before speed and the prefabricated house became an unfortunate part of our daily lives. Who can look at such pictures as *Continental Street-Scene*, *The Leaning Tower*, *Bologna* and *Florence*, with their bright crowds of market people, and at *Honfleur*, without a *nostalgia* for the world before the 'triumph' of the machine?

CONTINENTAL STREET SCENE

WILLIAM CALLOW

Signed W. Callow, 1847.

By permission of the Laing Art Gallery, Newcastle-upon-Tyne.

[10½ × 14 in.]

WILLIAM JAMES MUELLER

1812–45

THERE is no ending to the skill of William James Mueller. Son of a German who escaped from Germany during the Napoleonic wars and became curator of the Museum at Bristol, Mueller as a boy showed that remarkable facility of expression which is his chief gift. Nor is it wise to assume that Mueller is merely the brilliant technician whose powers of rapid improvisation staggered David Cox when this master water-colourist went to Mueller for oil painting lessons in 1839. Mueller's range, if we consider so subtle a water-colour as *St. Peter's Hospital, Bristol,* in the Laing Collection, and so large and powerful an oil painting as *The Old Mill at Dolgarrog, presented* by Mr F. J. Nettlefold to the Birkenhead Art Gallery, is more than creditable. One is constantly being surprised by some work by Mueller which proves dexterity in a *different* kind of subject. He was primarily a landscape painter, and the richness and lucidity of his colouring anticipates the impressionist school. Like so many artists of his time Mueller was a great traveller in search of subjects. He knew England and Wales intimately, and some of his best drawings are of picturesque scenery, pastoral and mountain. While a very young man he visited Germany, Switzerland and Italy. In 1834 he was in Greece and Egypt. In 1843–4 he accompanied Mr (afterwards Sir) Charles Fellows on his expedition to Lycia, and brought back a large number of sketches of Oriental life. When we remember that Mueller was only thirty-three when he died, and that his health during the last years of his life was anything but robust, the quantity as well as the quality of his work is a problem of considerable interest. Like other geniuses who died young—Girtin, Bonington—like Thomas Collier, who died at a precarious fifty, Mueller may have been aware of limited time. Hence his perpetual energy.

INTERIOR OF THE CHANCEL OF THE COLLEGIATE CHURCH OF
ST PAUL'S, ANTWERP

WILLIAM JAMES MUELLER

By permission of the City Museum and Art Gallery, Birmingham.

[24⅜ × 18 in.]

THOMAS COLLIER

R.I., CHEVALIER OF THE LEGION OF HONOUR

1840–91

WRITING to his friend Charles Stuart Millard on November 15, 1864, Thomas Collier remarks that he had 'a drawing on hand of the Lledr Valley—a rasper. There was a great spree here on the fifth. We had no end of fireworks and a good guy and bonfire, the ceremony, of course, concluding with a grand liquoring up. . . .' The letter is typical of Collier's literary style, the expression 'rasper' probably signifying his pleasure in the progress of his drawing. One of the least known and one of the greatest of water-colourists, the artist's professional life coincided with a bad period of the art. He, however, went back to the ideals of the old masters of water-colour, while his contemporaries involved themselves in the fashionable expedients of high finish and artificial subjects. Collier looked back to Girtin, Constable, de Wint and David Cox, and the five years that he spent near Bettws-y-Coed from 1864 to 1869 were the foundation of his career as an artist. He came to live in London in 1871, and was made a member of the Institute of Painters in Water-Colours in 1872. In 1879 he built a large neo-Georgian house with a studio at Hampstead Hill Gardens, and named it Etherow in memory of a stream near Glossop, Derbyshire, where he was born. He had married in 1865 Miss Hermione Beatrice Holdstock by whom he had a son and a daughter. Mrs Collier died before the London house was completed, and the artist eventually married Miss Jessie Ida Tawell. In certain respects, particularly in regard to sky-painting, his art is unsurpassed. James Orrock, artist and connoisseur, wrote that 'it is not too much to say that "Tom" Collier was the finest of sky painters, especially of rain and cumulus clouds, while possessing more mastery of direct modelling and pearl grey shadows than any of our brotherhood. . . . In moorland with brilliant skies full of "accident" he never had a rival. . . .' He could do large water-colours from sketches in his studio with such atmospheric truth that they had the appearance of having been done in the open air. Collier's work was greatly admired in his day, and had he wished he could have been President of the Royal Institute of Painters in Water-Colours, but declined the honour. The artist, whose health was always delicate, died of consumption on May 14, 1891.

STACKING PEAT, FESTINIOG, NORTH WALES

THOMAS COLLIER, R.I.

Signed Thomas Collier, 1881.

Formerly in Mr F. J. Nettlefold's Collection, and presented by him to the National
Library of Wales.

[19½ × 29½ in.]

FREDERICK WALKER

A.R.A., R.W.S.

1840–75

H E WAS 'poignantly sensitive to all kinds of impressions, as well as to those of the lovely looks of human beings and aspects of the world which he has put on record for us. Music went through and through him. He was excessively tender to animals. The same intense and vibrating sensitiveness passed into his personal relations. One felt towards him almost as towards woman or child, because of his small stature, his delicate hands and feet and quick emotions, as well as because of a look there was in his eyes like the wistful and liquid looks of children. . . . He has gone to the undiscovered country, and we are left to mourn for many a fair vision unrealized.' So wrote Sidney Colvin in the *Cornhill Magazine* for July 1875. Fred Walker was among those beloved of the gods, for he died young, but not before he had enriched the world with some of the loveliest drawings ever made, showing technical mastery and a grave love of the visible beauty of the universe, infused with a deep spiritual recognition of its divine origin. I have always regarded Fred Walker as a religious painter, though his work was devoted not to religious subjects but to simple human themes wherein the beauty of women and children and the brave, natural dignity of men shine through as with a golden light. Though his style was minutely finished, it was not for the sake of detail only that he plodded and struggled, redrew and revised from scores of preliminary notes and sketches before something emerged approximating to his fastidious ideal. For Walker was never satisfied. His mind was an essentially poetic one, and the immortal lyric is inherent in all his compositions. Youth, Age, Love, Time and Death can be dimly discerned behind the realistic arrangements which form his groups of figures, with or without their landscape settings. Maybe the artist's own fragile health intensified his longing for life and art and his apprehensions of death. Greatly admired by his contemporaries, Fred Walker left them all subdued when his life came to its premature end. George Frederick Watts, in the garden of his Kensington house, discussing art in general with Herbert Granville Fell, took into his hands a vernal spray of leaf and flower. 'Look at this,' he said. 'How beautiful it is, and how few artists try to paint it properly. Think how Fred Walker would have done it!'

THE OLD GATE

FREDERICK WALKER, A.R.A., R.W.S.

Painted 1874-5. The artist's last exhibited water-colour.

By permission of the Tate Gallery.

[9¾ × 12¼ in.]

125

SIR GEORGE CLAUSEN

R.A., R.W.S.

1852–1944

BORN IN 1852, George Clausen started his career as an artist when painting in England was anything but distinguished. Turning his back on the current of popular art, he soon 'arrived' as a painter with a true vision of nature. For some time in the studio of that fine landscape painter, Edwin Long, he also studied the figure under Bouguereau and Fleury in Paris. He was influenced by Bastien Lepage, and, equipped with technical powers equal to his dreams, Clausen was conspicuous for his pastoral scenes enlivened with charming but essentially natural figures of peasants. Made a member of the Royal Society of Painters in Water-Colours in 1898, a Royal Academician in 1908, and knighted in 1927, he was never content to rest on his laurels and, as so many other painters, to repeat his successes over and over again. In fact, Clausen was always studying, experimenting and seeking for fuller expression of his ideals. Tolerant of all that was good in modern painting he was equally intolerant of ugly, insincere and fraudulent mannerisms. In every sense of the word a complete artist, Clausen found all aspects of nature from landscape to figures and faces, subjects for interpretation, but where he differed from some of his Victorian contemporaries was in his power to find 'under the common thing the hidden grace', and to reveal beauty where one would least expect to find it. In water-colour painting, particularly, during the last twenty years of his life, he took the old themes of trees and atmospheric effects and gave them a new kind of aesthetic verity, drawing them with great breadth of style. As a man, Clausen, like most men who achieve greatness in art, was modest to a degree, always willing to listen encouragingly to the sincere young aspirant, and to help him along the difficult road. He died at the great age of ninety-two, honoured and respected by artists all over the world.

THE SHOWER
SIR GEORGE CLAUSEN, R.A., R.W.S.

By permission of the Fine Art Society, Ltd..
$[9\frac{1}{4} \times 11\frac{1}{2}$ in.]

W. J. WAINWRIGHT

R.W.S.

1855 1931

AN ARTIST well-beloved and respected in his native Birmingham, Wainwright had something of the integrity and deep human sympathy of the great David Cox, also a Birmingham man; and Wainwright's posthumous portrait of Cox was obviously one that he enjoyed doing. At the age of fourteen he was apprenticed to John Hardman and Co., art workers chiefly in stained glass. In 1880 he went to Antwerp and studied at the Royal Academy there. In 1881 he was in Paris. Then followed periods in London and Newlyn, and finally he settled in Birmingham, taking a keen interest in the culture of the city. A conscientious draughtsman, he held the view, shared by the Old Masters, that sketches, however robust and brilliant, were merely the means to a finished picture, and he never exhibited anything that did not completely fulfil his intentions as regards a combination of effect and detail. In this age when the sketch is often praised beyond its deserts, Wainwright's idea of finish is apt to be unpopular with the intellectuals of art, but for every artist who can carry through a conception to its end, there are scores who can make the embryonic note. The charm of Wainwright's character is revealed in the late Walter Turner's devoted study of the artist, published in 1935. A friend to all, Wainwright in turn won everybody's affection and respect. His models, particularly old Findon, a Crimean veteran, liked to work for him. It was Findon's pride to assist the artist. We learn that 'on one occasion when Findon was sitting for Falstaff he entered into the part so zealously and with so much spirit that the smile on his round rubicund face developed slowly but surely with greater intensity until it was transformed into an uncontrollable fit of laughter. He remained like that,' writes Wilfrid Wainwright, 'until my father put down his palette and laughed heartily at the sight of him. Tears were rolling from poor old Findon's eyes from sheer delight and content. He was really so happy in the studio and loved his task—trying with all his might to enter into the part to the best of his ability.'

SANCHO PANZA

W. J. WAINWRIGHT, R.W.S.

From the late Walter Turner's Collection.

[30½ × 21½ in.]

ARTHUR MELVILLE

R.W.S.

1855–1904

I F AN artist can so impress his personality on his medium as to make his work distinctive he has justified himself. The tradition of painting is capable of infinite variations, but to demand the completely original style and the absolutely new vision is a theoretical affectation. It is this attitude which brings chaos and chicanery into the visual arts, and rewards incompetence and insincerity with money and fame. Arthur Melville, born in 1855, began to practise his art in the 'seventies, a bad period for water-colour painting. Detail, stipple and trivial subjects were the order of the day, but Melville did not revolt against the tradition and produce incomprehensible pictures. He merely found a method of expressing life in a fresh and exciting way. While we are aware that Melville was doing something different from the usual run of work at the time, we do not need a long and involved literary explanation of the picture or the aims of the artist. Melville was an impressionist, but his method of handling rich, sensuous colour in a 'blottesque' way and bringing a pattern to coherence out of a confusion of tints cannot have been very different from that of Peter de Wint, except that Melville soaked his drawing paper first with Chinese white. His object was to reveal brilliant contrasts of light and shade, colour and movement of the Oriental and Spanish scene. Like Thomas Collier, he was one of the greatest sketchers, concerned always with the general effect rather than with detail, but his brief and nervous style, especially with crowds, is never empty and insignificant. He was not an impeccable draughtsman, but the most accurate drawing could not give us a better idea of the colour, the heat, the courage, cruelty and passion of such a subject as *The Little Bull Fight: Bravo Toro!* one of Melville's best works, in the Victoria and Albert Museum. His understanding of the Spanish scene and the magic and mystery of the Orient is all the more remarkable in that he was racially remote from those hot and dusty lands, having been born at Loanhead-of-Guthrie, Forfarshire; but he became as it were an immortal dragoman of art interpreting the Oriental world in a lucid language that can be understood by everybody. *Waiting for the Sultan* is also a conspicuously fine example of Melville's work.

WAITING FOR THE SULTAN

Arthur Melville, R.W.S.

Signed and dated 1891.

By permission of the National Gallery of Scotland.

[21¼ × 30⅛ in.]

131

ALFRED WILLIAM RICH

1856–1921

ONE OF Orpen's best portraits (he, himself, would have described it as an 'Orps', thereby signifying that he was not displeased with it), was of Alfred William Rich. With a bright, red, open-air face, a shock of white hair, holding a palette on a brawny arm, it is very like Rich, expressing something of the sturdy independence of the Sussex man determined on his own course of action. In Rich's case, this course was to combine the old traditions of water-colour painting to be seen in de Wint and Cotman with his own attitude. Rich was a good sketcher, improvising on nature, but never beyond our experience of visual truth. He was first apprenticed to wood-engraving and then became a heraldic draughtsman and illuminator, but his feeling for landscape and the use of the large sable brush were too strong for him to remain a slave to the graver. It was not, however, until he was thirty-four that he went to study Fine Art at the Slade School, a good moment, for the Slade and the New English manner were of great help to Rich in finding himself. He reserved his work for New English exhibitions and was a regular exhibitor from 1896 until the end of his life. He also showed at the short-lived but influential International Society, and at provincial exhibitions. His drawings, even the least effective, are stimulating for a certain audacity of style, and are very English in their appreciation of our uncertain climate. Rich was also one of the best teachers of modern times, and his annual sketching tours were the occasion for a reunion of students in some favourite part of the countryside. He worked until the last trying to help others to see in landscape what he could see, and it was while conducting a class at Tewkesbury that he caught a chill and died from pneumonia on September 7, 1921. Miss H. R. Lock has written a sympathetic account of Rich's life in one of Mr Augustus Walker's *Quarterlies*. Rich wrote a valuable book on painting in water-colours.

ROCHESTER

ALFRED WILLIAM RICH

By permission of the Fine Art Society, Ltd.

[10 × 15 in.]

133

JOHN SINGER SARGENT

R.A., R.W.S.

1856–1925

THE BEST story of Sargent, as revealing the character of the man, is the one about the painter and the farmer. Sargent was sketching in a field when he was ordered off by a bullying farmer—a heavyweight. The artist went. When in town, however, he took some boxing lessons. Some time later Sargent returned to that very field and went on with his work. He was menaced again by that same farmer, whereupon Sargent, knowing something about the art of boxing, put up a 'good show' and the farmer retreated, leaving the artist in possession. Technique, in all things, was of great importance to this splendid American, and it is probably his immense skill and *bravura* which have reduced his reputation as an artist in an age when some artists have become famous for their ineptitude. The 'boom' and the bloom, for the time being, are off Sargent, for the simple reason that he was so accomplished, so strong and so healthy in his handling of life and art. When we recall his Memorial Exhibition at the Royal Academy, the acres of pictures, none bad, many very fine, we remember an artist determined on achievement. Sargent loved life and was devoted to art, and, though at times he found his position as premier portrait painter somewhat irksome, he was fascinated by the human comedy and tragedy as revealed in the faces, clothes and manners of his sitters. Coming to his water-colours, he took them as one tired of the noisy vanities of the world—the vast fashionable studio, the increasing number of clients, the financial and social obligations of the portrait 'game'—longing to play a little instrument of his own in some secluded beauty spot. His water-colours show all the strength of his portraits, the masterly drawing, the eagle eye for effect, the pugnacious stroke of the brush. Some of those of Venice, particularly, stand out a monument to his robust personality. Sargent died suddenly in his London studio, with a volume of Voltaire by his side.

VENETIAN CANAL
JOHN SINGER SARGENT, R.A., R.W.S.

By permission of Hugo Pitman, Esq.
[14 × 20 in.]

135

P. WILSON STEER

O.M.

1860–1942

TALL AND large in girth, inarticulate of speech and non-committal of physiognomy, Wilson Steer is one of the enigmas of the art world. While, in a sense, he was the apotheosis of Impressionism, strongly linked by time and training to the French School, he was fundamentally English in his vision of Nature. He had something of Constable, Turner and Richard Wilson in his sense of beauty, and plodded on until he reached the pinnacle of fame. Steer was the doyen of the New English Art Club, which he helped to found, and also of the Chelsea Arts Club, where he would sit of an evening with a kind of Oriental concentration on chess. When not there or at his house in Cheyne Walk, he was away sketching the English countryside. As a water-colour painter Steer takes a prominent place, not for the pictorial content of his subjects, but for his exquisite feeling, delicate colour and tone values. There are water-colours by Steer that look as if they had been blown by some kindly zephyr on to the drawing paper. He had a gift for suggesting rather than realizing an idea, and one cannot but admire his skill in eliminating all but the essential spirit of his theme. A few palings, an expanse of water and sky, a sailing barge, a group of trees in Steer's hands became a kind of evanescence, charming and mysterious like some elusive dream. He was a master of the 'blottesque' style of water-colouring which reminds one at times of Alexander Cozens, Peter de Wint or the remote Chinese. Within its limitations his work is perfect, and he knew those limitations and never attempted subjects beyond the power of his draughtsmanship in the water-colour method. Exclusive, detached from society and societies, except the New English, Steer possessed from boyhood that singleness of purpose that makes for ultimate achievement in art, and his long life was crowned with a fame and material success perhaps even beyond his own imaginings. He died in 1942, leaving a fortune of £114,000.

HAWES, LANCASHIRE
P. WILSON STEER, O.M.

Courtesy of Messrs Thomas Agnew & Sons, Ltd.
[10 × 14½ in.]

137

JOSEPH CRAWHALL

1861–1913

THERE is a portrait of Joseph Crawhall by A. S. Hartrick, with large dark brown eyes and eyebrows, a fringe covering the whole of his forehead, full lips and the suggestion of a moustache. Add a gold earring, and it would be the face of a Spanish gipsy. One cannot associate such a face with English squirearchy, with the Northumbrian house at Morpeth where Crawhall was born. His father had an estate at Rothbury, and was himself an amateur artist and friend of Charles Keene. His mother hailed from Scotland. What strange quirk in Crawhall's heredity produced one of the master draughtsmen of all time, albeit one of the least known to the world, and strangest of personalities? Among the older generation of living artists, Sir Alfred Munnings, Herbert Granville Fell and A. S. Hartrick, 'Creeps', as he was called by his friends, is still regarded with awe and not a little merriment. Fell can recall somewhat riotous evenings in King's Road, Chelsea, with an exceptionally convivial friend, who took his own genius as an artist for granted and saw nothing extraordinary about it. He was apparently more interested in hunting and good cheer. The best description of Crawhall is to be found in Cunninghame-Graham's essay entitled 'Creeps'. Indulging his instinct for wandering, Crawhall went to Tangier, where he introduced the English sport of foxhunting, and was second whip to a pack of hounds. Cunninghame-Graham astutely likens Crawhall's art to that of the draughtsmen of the Altamira caves, but it was infinitely richer and more accurate, if his methods were perhaps the same. No artist has drawn animals and birds with greater distinction. I am informed by an artist who saw him work that he would sit and watch his 'quarry' for half an hour or more and memorize. He would then retire to his studio in a creative frenzy, using the brush with such *premier-coup* precision as to render a living likeness of the object in his mind. Sir John Lavery in *The Life of a Painter* (1940) writes, 'In a few lines he could sketch an animal, making it more recognizable than the most candid camera could do. . . . If he did a pack of hounds the huntsman would be able to recognize every single one.' Cunninghame-Graham writes, 'Creeps suffered no pangs of parturition, and I remember once when someone said all art was difficult he answered simply, without a trace of boastfulness, "No, not at all." He never strove after originality, but painted as a bird sings, without a thought of the effect it makes. . . .'

THE GREYHOUND
Joseph Crawhall

By permission of the Glasgow Art Gallery.
[14½ × 14½ in.]

FRED ROE

R.I.

1864–1947

THE MIDDLE-AGED can remember with what delight they followed the career of Fred Roe in their youth. His pictures of Nelson and other historical figures and scenes were always prominent at the Royal Academy. They were drawn and painted in a vivid realistic style, with great knowledge of costume and characterization, for Roe was a careful student of history. Maybe it was the curious fact that his father was born in the eighteenth century that accounted for the artist's instinct for historical scene, an instinct that stimulated his imagination and gave his works an authority beyond the ordinary illustrative effort. He was a member of the school of historical and genre painters, like Seymour Lucas and Ernest Crofts, who were immensely popular in late Victorian and in Edwardian days; and he was to live to see that school temporarily abolished by theoretical aberrations. Roe, however, was not deflected in his course by the trend of events in art, but pursued his objective and made many records of the first and second World Wars. Thus his work as a whole is concerned with the ardours and endurances of youth caught in the tumult of their times, whether past or present. His dramatic sense was ever on the alert for subjects appropriate to his muse. His work, in effect, is a period piece, and period pieces have a habit of surviving the fashionable canvas. But Roe was also a landscape-painter of quality, and certainly a pencil draughtsman of exquisite touch. His antiquarian interests concentrated his attention on old masterpieces of architecture and furniture and his *History of Old Oak Furniture, Ancient Church Chests and Chairs round Greater London, Essex Survivals,* and *Vanishing England* are classics. I think Fred Roe was the youngest ancient I was ever privileged to know. Tall, broad and physically very strong, he looked about sixty, but was in fact eighty-three when he died. It was only during the last few weeks of his life that he complained of feeling somewhat tired. I was with him and his son, Gordon Roe, almost immediately before the end, but though the fires of mortal life were ebbing away his spirit was bright and intense, and his mind was obviously on some work he proposed to do as soon as he could rise from his bed. The water-colour reproduced on the opposite page was his last work, drawn on the spot in the heat of the summer of 1947, just before he died.

RED ROOFS AT WEST WYCOMBE

FRED ROE, R.I.

By permission of F. Gordon Roe, Esq., F.S.A.

[13 × 18½ in.]

A. S. HARTRICK

R.W.S.

b. 1864

ONE OF the best books ever written by an artist is Mr Hartrick's bio-graphy, *A Painter's Pilgrimage through Fifty Years*. Hartrick's stars brought him into touch with Gauguin, Van Gogh and Toulouse-Lautrec, in the 'eighties and 'nineties; and he has inscribed some valuable memories of those *fauves* and left some rare portraits of them. As an illustrator, he knew the most prominent artists of his time—the exotic Beardsley, that master of line E. J. Sullivan, and the brilliant Phil May. Hartrick was on the staff of the newly founded *Daily Graphic*, and his and Sullivan's names were among the first to be entered on the list of members of the Chelsea Arts Club. He writes with authority about such vital movements as the foundation of the New English Art Club, and the International Society of Sculptors, Painters and Engravers. During a long life Hartrick has enjoyed many contrasts and met innumerable celebrities in art. He has the gift of adapting himself happily to town or country, but perhaps the happiest time was at Tresham in the Cotswolds, where he lived for about ten years—years that produced his memor-able series of drawings of Cotswold types and customs. Hartrick, like Sullivan, was one of the best teachers of his time, and many of the younger men are grateful to him for having led them into virtuous paths of good, honest drawing. I am in entire agreement with him that too much theory *à la* Roger Fry and his literary descendants, has done infinite harm to creative art. As it is pertinent to the theme of water-colour painting, I quote from his chapter, 'London Again'. 'In the spring of 1908 the stars must have been regarding me and my efforts with kindly eyes. . . . Anyway, in March I was elected an Associate of the Royal Society of Painters in Water-Colours. . . . Being frankly an individualist in art, painting just as I can, and often not as I would, I must often, by my experiments, have shocked the eyes that guard the Society's portals. I fancy Clausen and Arthur Rackham, my proposer and backer, must have been bold to expect to persuade a majority to see that this work was certainly honest, and that I did know my business. Once a member, you are free, the equal of any, having justified yourself as artist to the majority. A better set of comrades I do not wish to meet, and now, as a veteran, I view the whole society simply with affection, as a band of brothers working sincerely for the benefit of their art.'

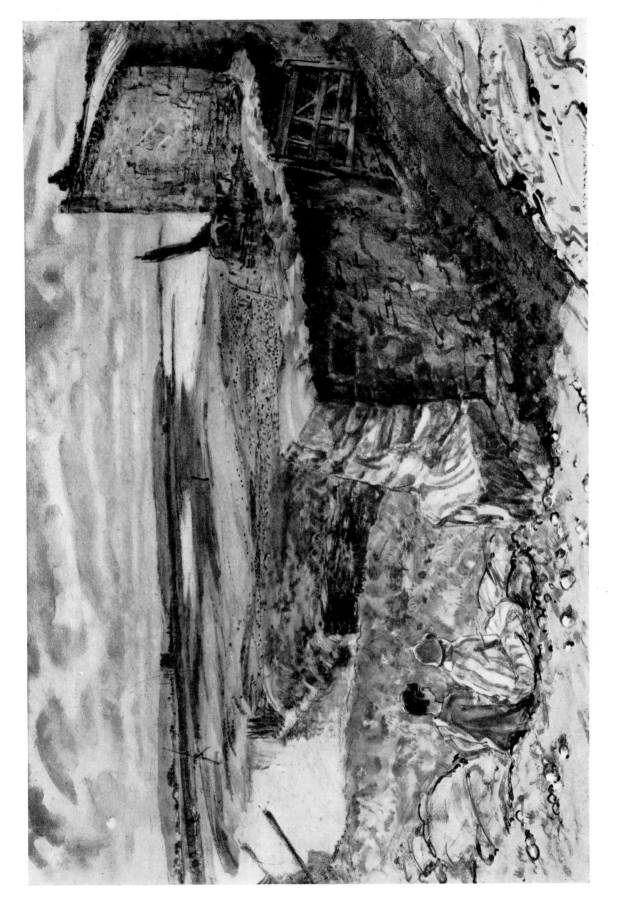

THE HARBOUR, OLD CLEVEDON, SOMERSET
A. S. HARTRICK, R.W.S.

By permission of Vincent Lines, Esq., R.W.S.
[15 × 21 in.]

ARTHUR RACKHAM

R.W.S.

1867–1940

To WIN the heart of the world's childhood is surely the sweetest of all successes. It is no exaggeration to say that Arthur Rackham did this. To do this is to have divination of the child-mind, given to few men. Lear and Lewis Carroll may be recalled, Charles Lamb and Kate Greenaway, and James Barrie to a lesser extent. Arthur Rackham, I venture to say, was the most appealing of all, in that his drawings were as lovely as the very children he drew, touching an ideal of happiness that is everybody's dream. One returns again and again to their inimitable grace, and is always refreshed by it. But it is not only the eternal child in his drawings that moves us, but the simple, imaginative, juvenile vision of a world of beauty and wonderment. Rackham could think as a child and invested his drawings for children with that magic which, alas, so soon departs. Even at his most grotesque Rackham is never frightening. Children delighted as much in his weird trees, with their suggestion of faces and arms, as in the normal interpretation of boys and girls, for the artist verified the childish fancy. To be fearfully thrilled is not really to be frightened, and I doubt if Rackham, at his most extravagant, ever alarmed any child. As an illustrator the artist began his career at a time when new ideas and techniques in reproduction had become available, and he organized his mental and technical powers for colour printing by the process method. He studied at the Lambeth School of Art, and his first great influence was Dalziel's edition of the *Arabian Nights*, illustrated by Arthur Boyd Houghton. Like other famous illustrators he worked for a while in Fleet Street, where he was attached to the *Westminster Gazette*. But before the end of the nineteenth century he began that series of illustrations for the classics and contemporary literature that was to bring him success and fame. A modern Puck, he put a girdle round the world, and won admiration from the multitude as from the individual collector. Mr A. S. Hartrick, in the *Old Water-Colour Society's Club*, Volume XVIII, writes: 'I remember his pleasure when relating to me his experience on a visit to see the collection of an important connoisseur in Paris, when his host, producing a key on a chain from his pocket, solemnly unlocked a safe to show his guest a specially framed drawing of his, which was evidently considered too precious to be hung on a wall.'

THE INCOMING TIDE
Arthur Rackham, R.W.S.

By permission of Mrs C. D. Rackham.
[15½ × 16¼ in.]

A. C. INCE
b. 1868

THE SLADE SCHOOL in the 'nineties must have been an adventurous place, for under the guidance of Legros and Fred Brown it discovered a host of talented artists and some who achieved a deserved fame. John, Orpen, Eves and McEvoy were a few of the celebrities who graduated from Gower Street, and the tradition of fine and sincere drawing was continued under Professor Tonks and Professor Schwabe. One of the most promising students in those days was Miss A. C. Ince, and it was hoped that her work would eventually place her in the forefront of artists. Miss Ince, however, was unable to fulfil this promise on account of ill-health and failing eyesight. With complete blindness in one eye and such short sight in the other, she abandoned the struggle as hopeless for many years, and had to content herself with a mental rather than visual appreciation of art and nature. Being unable to read, she had perforce to employ people to read to her, mostly about the world of art, and biographies of artists. It was not until she was sixty that she made some tentative efforts to paint again, and after a while concentrated on flowers. These had to be placed within a few inches of her less defective eye. To distinguish the various colours the artist had to bend her head right over the palette. Notwithstanding this handicap Miss Ince worked for some hours daily over a period of years, doing hundreds of impressions with a large brush full of colour. Encouraged by her friends, among whom were certain well-known artists, Miss Ince achieved a position as a flower painter, held several exhibitions and contributed to various provincial shows. Only her intimates were aware of the grave disability under which she painted. Nor could she herself see the quality of her work and had to take on trust the praise of those who followed her brave efforts. Her case, I venture to say, is unique in the annals of art. Nobody looking at her flower pieces, so strong in impressionistic drawing, so rich in colour, and so direct in style, could imagine that the artist was to all intents and purposes sightless, so blind in fact that she could not recognize a friend seated opposite her at the dinner table. Her work surely comes into the category of inspiration, but inspiration founded on intense study in her youth, and an inner devotion to the beauty of flowers which she divines rather than sees.

ROSES IN WHITE BOWL
A. C. INCE

[11 × 13½ in.]

OLIVER HALL

R.A., R.W.S.

b. 1869

THE QUIET, restrained dignity of a landscape by Oliver Hall reminds one of Richard Wilson's mood—a mood often serenely in harmony with Nature herself. There is no obvious striving for effect, no startling colour. Oliver Hall does not impose his own idea on nature, but allows nature to lead him into the mystery. He was encouraged in his youth by his uncle, D. A. Williamson, follower of the Pre-Raphaelites and later of David Cox. Williamson, living at Broughton-in-Furness, helped to stimulate Oliver Hall's interest in landscape, for he began painting trees and moorland subjects in the neighbourhood of Ulverston and Bardsea Forest, places well known to David Cox and Thomas Collier. He also studied etching, and his early plates brought him a certain notoriety as an etcher and a limited income, sufficient, in fact, to enable him to marry at the age of thirty. After Oliver Hall's first one-man show at the Dowdeswell Gallery, his success as a landscape painter was assured. Although he has painted much in France and Belgium, the north English country still remains his real love. *Shap Moors*, a canvas of his middle period, was bought under the Chantrey Bequest for the Tate Gallery. Though he is principally a painter in oils, Oliver Hall's water-colours are none the less instinct with fine drawing and sensitive colour. So fresh and strong are they, even now when the artist is eighty years old, that we realize how truly devoted he has been all his life to certain ideals. Maybe the beauty of these late works is due, in part, to a tragic accident which destroyed his studio and most of its contents by fire in 1945. It was not by enemy action but from some cause never discovered. His painter-son, Claude Muncaster, was on the spot in a matter of minutes. There he discovered the old man searching disconsolately among a heap of sodden and still smoking water-colours, the only remnants, some thirty in number, of a life's work. As he observed his son approaching he threw up his hands in a gesture of despair, and dropping them to his sides turned away his head and wept. But in less than five minutes he recovered himself. 'Well,' he said, 'it's no use crying over spilt milk. If I were a younger man perhaps I would care more. Now . . . well . . . I'm just going to sit down and paint better than I've ever painted before!' And he has done.

WOODLAND TRACERY

OLIVER HALL, R.A., R.W.S.

[9½ × 14¼ in.]

149

EDGAR THOMAS HOLDING

R.W.S.

b. 1870

HOLDING was born in Hornchurch, Lincolnshire, and in early life was connected with business; but soon found his real life, that of an artist. For many years he has made his home at the foot of the Sussex Downs, and has devoted himself to expressing the Sussex scene. He has painted it in all lights and weathers. Being essentially a poet of nature, Holding revels in rustic sentiment, and expresses it in a broad and lucid style. One of the best things ever written about the art he professes fell from his pen with the same eloquence as that with which he lays in his trees, pastures and downs with the brush. He wrote: 'The practice of this gentle art has led me nearer to paradise and the eternal truths and beauties of life than any other my feet have trod. It does not matter in the least that the song has been feeble, that it has not really expressed the vision that the beauty evoked. The great Critic, knowing the hearts of his children, values only the spirit that moves them—sees the motive rather than the achievement—and measures our stumbling efforts by standards unknown in the market-place. The art of water-colour is inseparately associated in my mind with all that is beautiful in this land of my birth. To praise water-colour is for me to praise England, and to be for ever indebted to those painters who have shown me by their work how beautiful our land is, and how perfect a medium water-colour may be for giving expression to that beauty.' Holding was made an Associate of the Royal Society of Painters in Water-Colours in 1920, and a full member in 1929. For many years he was the Society's efficient and courteous Honorary Treasurer, retiring in 1949. His water-colours appear in important public and private collections.

BIGNOR DOWN, SUSSEX
EDGAR THOMAS HOLDING, R.W.S.

By permission of C. H. James, Esq., R.A.
[12½ × 19¼ in.]

LESLIE BADHAM

R.B.A.

1873–1945

EW TOWNS have been fortunate in possessing a Leslie Badham to make thousands of drawings of local pictorial interest. The artist, domiciled for years at Hastings, might be described as the 'Unofficial Recorder of Hastings'. He would sit for hours every day doing careful studies of the 'ancient monuments', quaint corners and streets of villas. Sometimes one would find Badham in the fisherman's quarter, extracting colour and grace from the luggers, or mystery from the gaunt characteristic black huts where the nets are dried. He would go up to Fairlight, or Eastbourne way, and do a panoramic view. He would spend his leisure in making model boats. All this, when he was not teaching at the Hastings School of Art. To be with Badham, looking for a subject to sketch, was to be aware of a young personality in an elderly frame. Although the artist must have been nearly seventy when I first met him, with his keen eye, full of hope and optimism, and quick movements, he might have been a young man. His studio, not far from the sea, was a genial and cosy place full of drawings and an excellent art library; but it was only with persuasion that one could induce Badham to show his own works, for, diffident to a degree, he would much rather talk about somebody else's, or take out an Old Master sketch that he had just picked up in one of the curiosity shops of the town. 'That's a nice little Constable drawing,' I would say. 'Yes,' answered Badham with a rapturous look. 'Fifteen shillings. I never pay more than a pound for an Old Master.' I had been down to Hastings for twenty-four hours. It had been a week-end of bombing. The warnings were going all day and night. Badham saw me off at the station, and I noticed that he was somewhat quiet. 'I suppose you're seeing it through,' I remarked, on saying 'goodbye', thinking that he and his wife and daughter deserved rest in a less dangerous place. 'We're not moving,' Badham replied, 'we've stuck it all through. The end can't be far off now.' A few weeks afterwards, glancing at an evening paper, I read, 'Leslie Badham, the well-known artist, was killed as a result of enemy action.' His house had received a direct hit. His daughter died with him, and his wife died soon afterwards. But his happy and ingenious spirit lives on in the drawings purchased by the Town Council for their permanent collection.

FISHING LUGGERS

LESLIE BADHAM, R.B.A.

By permission of the Hastings Museum and Art Gallery.

[$10\frac{3}{4} \times 14\frac{3}{4}$ in.]

CHARLES SIMS

R.A., R.W.S.

1873–1928

KEEP A 'Heavenly heart to govern your vision, but take all Earth's kindliness, jollity, style, and misadventure, and paint the best of what you can see. Use Earth as a hunting ground for subjects; at times Earth is Heaven, try to capture these moments. Say not Earth may be Heaven, but Earth *is* Heaven at times.' So wrote Charles Sims, and the artist's attitude to life and to art could not have been better expressed. He was endowed with an excess of *joie de vivre*, and an enthusiasm for all things in nature. I regard some of his water-colour studies with the mother-and-child motif as among the loveliest things ever achieved in this medium. Such a drawing as the young mother reclining on a bed playing with her infant is truly religious in its response to the ideal of youth, beauty and motherhood. Many of Sims's pictures, in water-colours or oils, are concerned with the physical beauty of women and children. That the artist must have been intensely happy in his years at Fittleworth and Lodsworth in Sussex, studying nature and using his own children as models for those themes that made him famous, is obvious in his work. 'The game of loveliness is waiting to be played.' Such ideals are temporarily out of fashion, but they will come back into art as into life, for humanity cannot exist without them. Perhaps it was because Sims lived at such an altitude of joy, in such warmth and fealty, so exultingly, that contrast inseparable from human experience was all the darker when it came so tragically to complete his earthly destiny. Towards the end of his life all his joys seemed to be eclipsed, and his despair was expressed in a series of startling, abstract paintings which reveal the storm in his mind. Sims let go his hold on life, but left to posterity the enduring evidence of a fine and noble mind.

MOTHER AND CHILD
CHARLES SIMS, R.A., R.W.S.

By permission of the Laing Art Gallery, Newcastle-upon-Tyne.
[22 × 30½ in.]

CECIL A. HUNT

M.A., LL.B., R.W.S.

b. 1873

Cecil Hunt practised at the bar until 1919, and only transferred to the profession of art in that year on becoming an Associate of the Royal Society of Painters in Water-Colours. He had, however, devoted a great deal of his leisure time to painting, and was a member of the Royal Society of British Artists as early as 1914. During the first World War his legal abilities found scope in connection with certain political problems arising out of that war. Hunt's literary skill ranges from such themes as *Tudor on Charities, Bunyan on Life Assurance, Halsbury's Laws of England,* and conveyancing, to his *Stories of English Artists.* This duality of temperament is specially interesting at a time when artists are supposed and expected to specialize and devote all their energies to painting, and proves that, given the power to concentrate, one can so order one's life to succeed in more than one direction. There are few painters of mountain subjects, past or present, who have acquired so certain a knowledge of what Ruskin considered to be the most beautiful subject. Hunt has made a study of mountains in all parts of the world, and has their diversity of character at his finger-tips, as it were, for mountains, like human beings do have a 'racial' significance, whether our own homely peaks, the formidable Dolomites, the glacial Alps, the arid Sierras of Spain, or the Grand Canyon. The artist has made innumerable drawings in many parts of the world, always remembering that form or the anatomy of mountain scenery is indispensable to the true rendering of these superstructures. Thus a drawing by Cecil Hunt gives one a sense of the grandeur of the scene, and in this mood his work excels that of painters who are apt to emphasize picturesqueness and local colour.

SPANISH LANDSCAPE, ELVIRA

CECIL A. HUNT, M.A., LL.B., R.W.S.

[13¾ × 20 in.]

MARTIN HARDIE

C.B.E., R.E., R.S.W., Hon. R.W.S.

b. 1875

ARTIST, art-scholar and administrator, Martin Hardie is among the important figures in the world of water-colour art. Nephew of C. Martin Hardie, R.S.A., and on his mother's side of John Pettie, R.A., he was born in London in 1875. As a scholar at St Paul's School, he won several drawing prizes, and in 1895 became an Exhibitioner of Trinity College, Cambridge, taking an honours degree in the Classical Tripos in 1898. In that year he joined the staff of the Victoria and Albert Museum, and his career as an artist ran concurrently with his official work; it was, indeed, in the furtherance of technical knowledge that he studied etching and engraving under Sir Frank Short, and developed his practice of water-colour painting. He was Keeper of the Departments of Painting and of Engraving, Illustration and Design from 1914 till his retirement in 1935. Hardie's enthusiasm for the masters of water-colour is certainly reflected in the rearrangement which he inaugurated and in the many important additions made during his period of office to the magnificent national collection housed in the Museum. His own practice as an artist in this medium gives him special authority to discourse on its technical side, and nobody has done more to amplify knowledge of the art and the lives of our water-colourists. Hardie is a constant exhibitor at the Royal Academy and the Royal Society of Painters in Water-Colours, of which he is an Honorary Member. His writings on art, and particularly his contributions to the *Old Water-Colour Society's Club Volumes*, show vast knowledge of the subject and will prove of considerable aid to art historians of the future. Withal, Hardie has done active work for the Royal Society of Painter-Etchers since his election in 1907; was Vice-President of the Royal Institute of Painters in Water-Colours from 1934 to 1936; has served in honorary capacity on various other societies connected with the arts; and has helped in organizing many important exhibitions, including those held by the Royal Academy of British Art in 1934, and of Scottish Art in 1939. His publications include *John Pettie, R.A.; Frederick Goulding, Master-Printer of Copper Plates; Boulogne, a Base in France; Our Italian Front* (text by Warner Allen); *Samuel Palmer; Peter de Wint; J. S. Sargent; Charles Meryon; the Etching of James McBey;* and *The Etched and Engraved Work of Sir Frank Short.*

DERELICTS AT STROOD

MARTIN HARDIE, C.B.E., R.E., R.S.W., HON. R.W.S.

[10½ × 14½ in.]

159

THOMAS SHOTTER BOYS

1803–74

Notwithstanding the long wars culminating in Waterloo, it is a pleasant fact that English artists found the Continent, generally, a 'happy hunting ground' almost immediately after the fall of the first Empire. Before 1818, Frederick Nash had made a whole series of drawings of Paris. Bonington and Thomas Shotter Boys were there in the 'twenties, and both worked for *Voyages Pittoresques*, that sumptuous production in twenty-five volumes, sponsored by the French Government. Boys made his first appearance in the volume devoted to Languedoc, published in 1835, and he is represented in subsequent volumes. He had worked on the Continent for a long while, and acquired an accurate but also artistic style with medieval and contemporary architecture. In 1839 he produced *Picturesque Architecture in Paris, Ghent, Antwerp, Rouen,* etc., drawn from nature on the stone. Here are drawings that have 'crystallized' the romantic, medieval aspect of these cities before nineteenth-century changes were to renovate, not always for the better, their old faces. The drawings were reproduced in the then new method of chromo-lithography, and the book was highly praised. Following this success, Boys produced a work called *London As It Is,* though the London plates were coloured by hand and not by direct colour-printing. These drawings of London, having passed into oblivion for nearly fifty years after the artist's death, began to attract attention in the nineteen-twenties, both for their style, and as records of a London fast disappearing in the general rebuilding after the first World War. Nash's *Regent Street, Piccadilly from Old Bond Street, Hyde Park Corner,* and *Temple Bar,* with Londoners typical of their time, are delightful to contemplate in this age of speed, turmoil and bewildered crowds trying to escape death on the roads. Collectors admire these drawing now, as they did when first issued in 1842. But the artist must have gone out of fashion in mid-Victorian times. He died on October 10, 1874, in a lodging at 30 Acacia Road, St John's Wood, old, paralysed and obscure; but maybe he consoled himself with the reflection that nobody had ever done better drawings of old and new buildings, and that Louis Philippe had been so impressed by them that he had sent him a letter of praise and the present of a watch.

RIVER SCENE IN BELGIUM
THOMAS SHOTTER BOYS

By permission of Mrs I. J. Dunne.
[7 × 10¼ in.]

JOHN FREDERICK LEWIS

R.A.

1805–76

SOME artists toil for a lifetime to emerge at long last into recognition. John Frederick Lewis achieved all and more than all the fame he wanted by the age of twenty-one. He began by painting sporting subjects, and at the express wish of George IV resided in the neighbourhood of Windsor Castle. One of his pictures at that time is *Deer-Shooting in Windsor Forest, with Portraits of His Majesty's Head-Keepers,* exhibited at the Royal Academy in 1826. Suddenly tiring of society Lewis vanished from the scene, became a kind of aristocratic vagabond, wandered through Spain, Italy, North Africa, and finally settled for ten years in Egypt. Considerable mystery attaches to his life there. Certainly, he worked with great intensity at water-colour painting, and evolved a style unique for a combination of breadth and high finish. Maybe, like many men of genius, he worked by fits and starts, for Thackeray's description of Lewis, whom he visited in Cairo, suggests an Oriental *dolce far niente* rather than infinite and continuous capacity for taking pains. 'A man, in a long yellow gown, with a long beard somewhat tinged with grey, with his head shaved, and wearing on it first a white wadded cotton night-cap, second a red tarboosh, made his appearance and welcomed me cordially. . . . He shuffled off his outer slippers before he curled up on the divan before me. He clapped his hands and called "Mustapha". Mustapha came with more lights, pipes, and coffee. . . . As we talked, his Oriental coolness and languor gave way to British cordiality. . . . He has adapted himself outwardly, however, to Oriental life. When he goes abroad he rides a grey horse with red housings, and has two servants to walk beside him. He wears a very handsome grave costume of dark blue, consisting of an embroidered jacket and gaiters, and a pair of trowsers, which would make a set of dresses for an English family. His beard curls nobly over his chest, his Damascus scimitar on his thigh. . . . Here (in Cairo) he lives like a languid lotus-eater—a dreamy, hazy, lazy, tobaccofied life. . . . And even this life at Cairo was too civilized for him. The great pleasure of pleasures was life in the desert,—under the tents, with still *more* nothing to do than in Cairo. . . .' Is Thackeray's impression overdrawn? If not, when did Lewis find time to paint such pictures as moved Ruskin to lyrical ecstasy? 'I have never seen anything quite comparable to it reached by art,' he wrote of Lewis's picture *A Frank Encampment in the Desert.*

LIFE IN THE HAREM, CAIRO
John Frederick Lewis, R.A.

Signed and dated 1858.

By permission of the Victoria and Albert Museum.
[$23\frac{7}{8} \times 18\frac{3}{4}$ in.]

163

HERCULES BRABAZON BRABAZON

1821–1906

A COUNTRY squire, born the year after George IV came to the throne. A sensitive boy, he could take nothing seriously but sketching. And so he dabbled away his time, using a room in his Sussex house, Oaklands, Seddlescombe. 'Busy with his daubs,' as his relations would say. When he was not thus busy at Oaklands, he wandered the world from Paris to Venice and Rome, from Madrid to the Taj Mahal, making thousands of landscape notes, improvising on the Old Masters, always returning to Oaklands, always 'busy with his daubs'. When he was a young man, in the eighteen-forties, the years slipped away, the great events of the Victorian era passed him by. Middle-aged in the 'seventies, Brabazon went on, oblivious of the world, indifferent to social life, accumulating innumerable impressions of the things that interested him, a bowl of roses, a water-colour note of Goya's self-portrait, a shipwreck on the Sussex coast, a Moorish mosque, a Cumberland mountain. For recreation he liked music and talking about art. The autumn and winter of life came upon him, but Brabazon was endowed with some perpetual spring of youth. Artists, poets and children were his friends. Mrs R. G. Eves, widow of the celebrated portrait painter, tells me how as a child she used to creep away from the company and seek the old squire-water-colourist in his room, and with what mutual delight they would look through the 'daubs'. The world-acclaimed Sargent was sometimes of the company, and with difficulty induced Brabazon to have an exhibition, at the Goupil Gallery, the first public show of his pictures—Brabazon disliking the idea immensely. The exhibition was eventually opened. The rest is immortality. It was Sir Frederick Wedmore who wrote that Brabazon was 'a country gentleman who, at the age of seventy years old, made his début as a professional artist and straightway became famous'. Previously Ruskin had said: 'Brabazon is the only person since Turner at whose feet I can sit and worship and learn about colour.' Brabazon was, undoubtedly, a subtle colourist—in this respect as original and as distinguished as anybody can hope to be.

IMPROVISATION ON CONSTABLE'S PAINTING, THE HAYWAIN

HERCULES BRABAZON BRABAZON

By permission of Leonard Duke, Esq.

[9⅝ × 13½ in.]

165

MYLES BIRKET FOSTER

R.W.S.

1825–99

THE YEARS have not dimmed the halo of success which adorned Birket Foster during his lifetime. He was one of the most popular artists of the Victorian era, and notwithstanding the changes in art and social life since his death in 1899 Birket Foster's water-colours, judging by the prices they fetch in the sale-rooms, are now as much cherished by collectors as those of the great masters. That he is not among them aesthetically is certain, but there is something in his work that is irresistible to the average mind, and admirable even to those who can distinguish between the great and the not so great. Birket Foster was a detailist, and by dint of looking with a camera-like eye at nature, and by hard labour with small brushes, he was able to make a marvellous description of country scenes. It is one kind of truth, a visual aspect in which the leafy tree, the tangled hedge, the ruts in the road, the incidental and pretty figures of peasants, are rendered with microscopic verity. Birket Foster painted every roof-tile, every brick and stone, the wicker-basket, the cat and dog, the fleecy clouds—insisting on every fact, leaving nothing to the imagination. It is just because nothing is left to the imagination and there is no mystery in his work that Birket Foster only charms but fails to move us deeply. His scenes are too familiar, too like ordinary everyday experience. We know it all, we have seen it all. Only in so far as an artist can show us something that we don't know, and convince us that his vision is true, has he made an original contribution to art. None the less, Birket Foster was a supreme craftsman, and for this his work is to be respected. Like some of his contemporaries he was an expert wood-engraver. As a boy of sixteen he was apprenticed to Ebenezer Landells, a pupil of Bewick, and worked as an illustrator of books and for periodicals, but in 1858 he gave up this work for water-colour painting. *The Green Lane* is perfectly representative of his style. This work was probably done in the neighbourhood of Witley, Surrey, where Foster was domiciled for many years.

THE GREEN LANE
Myles Birket Foster, R.W.S.

Signed with monogram.

Formerly in Mr F. J. Nettlefold's Collection, and presented by him to the Diploma
Gallery of the Royal Society of Painters in Water-Colours.

[$17\frac{3}{4} \times 13\frac{3}{4}$ in.]

J. KERR-LAWSON

1864–1939

K ERR-LAWSON was born at Anstruther, Scotland, and went in early
childhood to Canada where he was educated, special attention being
given to the classics, so that when in his sixteenth year he found himself in Rome he was already an *initié*. Rome at that time was the Mecca for
painters, sculptors and men of letters from every part of Europe and America,
and the Café Greco was the rendezvous of all the wits and distinguished artists
then thronging the Eternal City. It was at this famous café that Kerr-Lawson
was introduced to Luigi Galli, the celebrated artist who became his master, from
whom he derived the broad principles of art that guided him throughout his
career, and under whose instruction he acquired the mastery of technique,
design and colour which distinguishes his work whether portraiture, landscape,
or mural decoration. In this latter form of painting he first exhibited at the
Alpine Club a series of panels of Italian subjects for the drawing-room of Mr
Christopher Turnor's house, Stoke Rochford, which made a great impression
in art circles, and led directly to a commission from the first Lord Aldenham
of a series of dramatic London scenes for a panelled library at Aldenham House.
These were not shown in London but went, like the greater part of Kerr-
Lawson's works, from his studio to their destined places. At the Beaux Arts
Gallery in 1942 there was a Memorial Exhibition where for the first time the
public had an opportunity of seeing the wide range of his accomplished works.
When Kerr-Lawson first went to Spain he walked straight into the pages of
Théophile Gautier's *Voyage en Espagne*, the land of Daniel Vierge, of George
Borrow and his Bible—into an unchanged Spain; and he, like them, caught
the many facets of this amazing land. Swiftly and brilliantly he recorded what
he saw of places and people; of mules and donkeys; of goats and gipsies. His
brush was never more vital, nor his touch surer than when painting amongst
the people he loved, and who affectionately spoke of him as *El Ingles mas
Andeluz*. Kerr-Lawson travelled much and lived in many countries from
Scotland to North Africa where he had many Moorish friends. The result
of his last stay in Morocco is three decorative panels of extreme beauty, *The
Mirage*, *The Water Wheel* and *The Café*, now in possession of Colonel A. C.
R. Waite, D.S.O. Other posthumous exhibitions of his work have been
given at the Hazlitt Gallery in 1947, the Beaux Arts Gallery in 1948, and at
Glasgow in 1949.

VENICE

J. KERR-LAWSON

By permission of Mrs Kerr-Lawson.

[11¼ × 18¾ in.]

169

WILLIAM THOMAS WOOD
R.W.S., R.O.I.

b. 1877

Most artists, given the will to work, can acquire in time a dexterous technique. If that were the one essential, art would cease to have any appeal to the cultured mind. While technique may excite envy, it is not enough, by itself, to awaken reverence. For this we must have the indefinable quality of mystery in a work of art, proving that the artist has vision to make his work memorable. I recall looking at two portraits, one by an artist justly famous throughout the world, the other by one not so famous. The first was impeccably drawn, technically beyond criticism, but it had little message for me beyond craftsmanship *in excelsis*. The second drawing was instinct with poetic feeling, and was therefore more than the literal transcript of physiognomical facts. It is this gift that places William Wood's work, whether figures, landscapes, or flowers, in a creative category. The artist looks beyond the surface of things, and invests them with an aura of grace. Whatever style he uses, whether highly finished drawings or such brief and rapid sky effects over downland country as can be seen on the opposite page, we are aware of a pensive mind in addition to an adroit hand. I once looked through a large sketch-book containing the preliminaries of many successful works by Wood. Artists' notes can be very stimulating, and sometimes better than the finished performances. In Wood's case, I felt that he had retained to a remarkable degree his original impulse when he adapted those works further for exhibition purposes. This is due to the fact that he has not allowed his technique to become a mannerism. Wood was made a member of the Royal Society of Painters in Water-Colours in 1918, and was its Vice-President from 1924 to 1927. He studied at the Regent Street Polytechnic and in Italy; and was Official War Artist in the Balkans, 1918. His book entitled *The Salonika Front* is of historic interest.

CUMULUS CLOUDS
W. T. Wood, R.W.S., R.O.I.

[15 × 18½ in.]

NORMAN WILKINSON

C.B.E., P.R.I., R.O.I., S.M.A.

b. 1878

LIKE George Chambers and Charles Bentley, Norman Wilkinson has devoted his life to marine painting. Ruskin regarded the sea as the most difficult of all subjects. Apparently formless and elusive to all who have not disciplined themselves to record it, the sea, like the human figure or any other department of nature, has structure and detail and of course infinite colour. In his direct and powerfully realized style, both in water-colour and oil, Wilkinson has added considerable knowledge to the old masters of marine subjects, particularly in regard to breezy colour-effects in which the sky plays a prominent part in the pictorial design. The artist's experience of ships of all kinds is profoundly professional, and quite a deal of his work is historically interesting. He has been a war-recorder in the two World Wars. It was Wilkinson who invented the method of dazzle painting, or camouflage, which was adopted by all the allied nations in the war of 1914–18, and he was adviser on camouflage to the Air Ministry, 1938–42. But the artist is also accomplished in subjects of general interest, and one of the finest poster artists of our time. To Wilkinson we owe many a pleasant vista in the murky atmosphere of urban life. Grey streets and dismal railway stations are not infrequently adorned with striking landscapes of beauty spots, reminding us that the British Isles are full of lovely and accessible places. Do we ever realize sufficiently how much the artistic poster has added to the pleasure of everyday life? While waiting for a train in many an industrial junction I have been refreshed by a vision of 'far other worlds and other seas', and found that it is a bold and colourful design by Norman Wilkinson. He is President of the Royal Institute of Water-Colour Painters, member of the Royal Institute of Oil-Painters, and Marine Painter to the Royal Yacht Squadron, as well as one of the founder-members of the Society of Marine Artists.

THE CONVOY

NORMAN WILKINSON, C.B.E., P.R.I., R.O.I., S.M.A.

[14 × 21 in.]

SIR WILLIAM RUSSELL FLINT

P.R.W.S., R.A., R.S.W.

b. 1880

FROM ITS foundation in 1804, the senior Society of Painters in Water-Colours has had ten Presidents, but none more distinguished or more versatile than Sir William Russell Flint. Born in Edinburgh in 1880, he graduated like several famous artists from illustrated journalism to the fine arts. As a young man he worked for four years on the doyen of weekly illustrated journals, the *Illustrated London News*, and in those days there was no finer or more exacting training for an artist. To deal graphically with the world's events needs uncommon resource, quickness of hand and mind, but it was not long before Sir William, by reason of his insistence on good figure drawing, was in the first flight of illustrators. His *Malory, Chaucer, Homer,* and *Theocritus* combine beauty of style with poetic feeling. Such then was the basis of this artist's mastery of figure work in water-colours; but, developing from illustration, he became the *painter* in this elusive medium, using a full brush of colour with unerring skill and effect. Among figure-painters in water-colour Sir William stands alone for directness of touch and luminosity, but needless to say his economy of treatment derives from profound knowledge of the human form. Throughout his life he has practised drawing the figure daily, with as much method as an expert pianist will practise the piano. Hence his groups and arrangements, in oil or water-colour landscapes, are always attractive in themselves. Not only for their technical brilliance but because the artist has an Hellenic sense of ideal form do they appeal to our love of what is appropriate and beautiful. In landscape, also, and particularly Scottish mountain scenes, Sir William expresses his gifts with the same clarity. Since his presidency of the Royal Society of Painters in Water-Colours (1937), this famous community has retained premier place, its exhibitions at Conduit Street, London, reminding one of the ageless dignity of an essentially British contribution to culture.

THE LAKE AND GROTTO

Sir William Russell Flint, P.R.W.S., R.A., R.S.W.

[13 × 21½ in.]

175

EVELYN CHESTON

1875–1929

THE WORK of Evelyn Cheston has yet to be recognized as among the finest water-colours of landscapes. When I saw her posthumous exhibition at the old galleries of the Royal Society of Painters in Water-Colours, in 1930, I was instantly aware of this. Their strength and breadth of handling, feeling for light and air under all climatic conditions, intelligent appreciation and simplification of form were a memorable experience. I can think of few women creative artists who offer the same subtle ecstatic joy in nature as Evelyn Cheston does. Mary Webb was among them. She, of course, was a writer, but both had a similar mystical vision of the universe. Evelyn Cheston's landscapes are all the more poignant since she suffered for many years from ill-health and defective eyesight, and we can well imagine the ordeal of so sensitive an artist in being threatened with blindness. The difficulties of sketching from nature are hard enough when one has radiant health and strong eyes, but Evelyn Cheston 'would take out half a dozen pairs of lenses in her little bag when working'; she would try them all and then despairingly say that they were quite hopeless. Discussing Thomas Collier, Frederick Wedmore says, 'the artist was struggling for years, as I remember, with death as well as art'. The same might be said of Evelyn Cheston. The *feu sacré*, which is the driving force of genius, supported her not in the vain ambition to shine as a great artist, but in her desire to reveal to the world—to share with humanity—the beauty of nature; and this she has undoubtedly done in the parcel of drawings that she has left to posterity. Evelyn Cheston looked at the world with tremendous interest and love for all its wonders.

LANDSCAPE
EVELYN CHESTON

By permission of Charles Sydney Cheston, Esq., R.W.S.
[10 × 14½ in.]

GERALD ACKERMANN

R.I.

b. 1876

AMONG our best sketchers of the sky is Gerald Ackermann. Like the sea, the sky is very difficult to interpret, its 'language' being superbly subtle and elusive. The artist once wrote that 'if you have painted a good sky you have produced a good picture'. Indeed, a good sky will redeem an otherwise ineffective drawing, but a bad sky will ruin the best of landscapes. Ackermann, for the purpose of convenience, may be called an impressionist, but he is really in the tradition of Peter de Wint and Thomas Collier. He goes directly to nature as they did, and his aim is to finish his water-colour at one sitting. With Ackermann's style such a procedure must be adopted if a truthful result is desired. Most water-colourists have known the disappointment of having left a fine sketch half finished, and returning to the subject next day only to find that the weather is changed, the light is different, and their interest and will to work confused. Very seldom do we see two skies alike. Nor is it possible to follow precisely the involutions of a sky in rapid movement. Simplification is therefore paramount if we are to get a realistic rather than a decorative effect. The charm of Ackermann's work is the apparently effortless effect of the result, as if blown upon the paper by the same wind that is moving the clouds across the heavens. For many years the artist has worked on the east coast at Blakeney, Suffolk, where he lives, and where the skies, always full of a fresh wind, accord with his particular vision and temperament. He has been in the habit of doing as many as a dozen quick notes of cloud effects in one morning. By constantly watching and striving with a large brush the artist has achieved a method which often renders the lucidity of the scene, a scene frequently of flat country, broad rivers and sailing craft, but he is equally successful with rustic subjects. Ackermann's appreciation of light, and tone values, is the key to his objective. If these are correct, detail is not essential to make a good water-colour. Ackermann was born at Blackheath, educated at New College, Eastbourne, and studied at Heatherley's and the Royal Academy Schools, where he won the Creswick prize and Landseer scholarship.

BLAKENEY

GERALD ACKERMANN, R.I.

By permission of the Fine Art Society, Ltd.

[9¼ × 14 in.]

AMBROSE McEVOY

A.R.A., R.W.S.

1878–1927

AMONG that company of brilliant students—William Orpen, Augustus John, Reginald Eves—who studied at the Slade School towards the end of the nineteenth century—was Ambrose McEvoy. He had a rare delicacy of feeling due perhaps to hereditary, environmental and physical tendencies. His self-portrait shows a sensitive face with a fragile hold on life; but like all consumptives his eyes were haunted with an urgency to live, to love and to learn. It was a fortunate chance that brought McEvoy, the boy, into touch with Whistler, for Whistler in his art had just that exquisite mood that found response in McEvoy's genius. McEvoy had much to do and little time in which to do it, but like Girtin, Bonington and Collier—all of whom died young—McEvoy followed the road to fame, avoiding the trials and errors of labyrinthine adventure. It was just before the first World War that he took the world by storm with portraits of beautiful women. To call them portraits is an understatement. They were more. These studies, either in water-colour or oil, were emanations. McEvoy has been described as the modern Gainsborough, and the comparison is not without some truth, though Gainsborough, of course, had more strength and power. The two artists' sense of feminine beauty however, had much in common. Confronted with a portrait by McEvoy we are in the presence of a harmonized balance of personalities—the artist's and the sitter's. Neither overwhelms the other's. These portraits are a collaborative effort, the result of exceptional sympathy and understanding. And it is a notable fact that McEvoy, unlike most portrait painters who have to fulfil commissions, often appeared to paint those faces and characters that he most wanted to paint. His studies in water-colour have a special place in this most difficult art, for his technique of drawing carefully with the pencil and then experimenting with blots of colour, 'washing in' and 'washing out' his effects until he had arrived at some preconceived excellence, was exclusive to himself.

PORTRAIT STUDY

AMBROSE McEVOY, A.R.A., R.W.S.

By permission of Mrs Anna Bazell.
[16½ × 11¾ in.]

SIR ALFRED J. MUNNINGS

P.R.A., Hon.R.W.S.

b. 1878

ONE OF the jolliest things ever written about open air sketching is Sir Alfred Munnings's essay in the *Old Water-Colour Society's Club Volume, 1931–2*. The President of the Royal Academy is too wise to try to tell us how to do it. Nobody can really explain the mystery in words, but Sir Alfred does, with a poet's insight, express the joy of the water-colourist, seated in a boat, perhaps in some East Anglian or Thames backwater, surrounded by the ever generous and beautiful gifts of Nature, 'willow trees silvering with the faintest breath of wind'. Then there is 'Meadowsweet along the river and grown up marsh dykes. Large dark green clumps of bulrushes are topped with brown sienna-coloured heads. . . . Water-hens with their little broods are clucking and scuttling in their forest of green sedges. Fleets of flat water-lily leaves on the water surface with golden cups gazing to the sky; one lovely cup by itself in mid-stream sits there anchored by its length of stalk going down to the green depths of the river bed where weeds sway in the current.' Every landscapist, every lover of nature, will echo Sir Alfred's sentiments, for whether we are famous or not the chief reward is in being able to commune with Nature, and to receive from her the peace that passeth all understanding. Sir Alfred Munnings is, of course, among the many distinguished artists in the school of English painting, and whether he is doing a vast canvas or a small water-colour his work has the authority of a master. He is in the true tradition of Stubbs, Ward, Constable and all those who enjoyed and expressed the happy, healthy life under our variable skies. It may be that Sir Alfred is the last great painter of equine subjects. We are in the jet-propelled era, and yet our great-grandfathers could remember when the horse was still the fastest means of travelling. Sir Alfred Munnings was born at Mendham in Suffolk, and studied at the Norwich School of Art; but his real studio has always been the open air. He was made President of the Royal Academy in 1944.

THE PASSING IMPRESSION

Sir Alfred J. Munnings, P.R.A., Hon.R.W.S.

By permission of Charles A. Hepburn, Esq.
[14⅜ × 20¾ in.]

ROBERT WORTHINGTON

R.F.C.S.

1878–1945

IT IS A notable fact that doctors, speaking generally, take kindly to art. I have already mentioned Dr Monro. Others include Sir Francis Seymour Haden, Whistler's brother-in-law, and Sir Gardiner Prescott Hewett, who were distinguished executants with the brush or pencil. Robert Worthington, also a surgeon, was devoted to landscape painting. He had sketched for many years, but it was after some lessons from Alfred Egerton Cooper that he evolved a style of impressionism which places Worthington with the good water-colourists of our time. An orderly mind gave him time during his busiest professional years to escape occasionally from the surgery to his supreme delight to sketching. To be with 'Bob' Worthington in his eyrie-like studio, a converted 1914–18 military hut on Dartmoor, was a memorable experience to artists and connoisseurs, for 'Bob' had made it a rendezvous where good company, good talk and excellent drawings were always available. I remember a week-end there going through Old Master drawings, Worthington putting them on the easel, and the test was our ability to identify the artists, not from signatures, but from styles. Nor was it inappropriate for Worthington to end this game by putting some of his own efforts up for our inspection, and the best of them were 'of the company'. It was Worthington's habit to travel about his surgeon's duties with colour-box and drawing paper, and here and there snatch an hour or even half an hour to do a sketch. Such limitation of opportunity gave a creative urgency to his style until he was able to do water-colour direct with the brush without the use of the pencil, rendering the essential atmospheric effect with untroubled washes of tint. The second World War, and Worthington's professional duties in connection with it, made sketching almost impossible, and it was that war which ruined his health. When it began, some of his friends, thinking Exeter where Worthington had a house would be beyond bombing range, sent their valuable pictures to him for safety. When Exeter was bombed on May 4, 1942, an incendiary bomb set fire to his house, and Worthington, careless of his own safety, toiled for hours trying to rescue his friends' treasures from the flames. He never recovered from this ordeal and died on July 11, 1945.

ON THE DART

ROBERT WORTHINGTON, F.R.C.S.

[10 × 14 in.]

WILLIAM SIDNEY CAUSER

R.I.

b. 1880

SOME artists are fortunate in deciding on the kind of work that suits their temperament, while being able to acknowledge the quality of other methods, styles and subjects. If Sidney Causer can admire the passionate and haphazard force of Van Gogh, he knows that his own gifts are as logical and as constructive as the architecture that he enjoys drawing—architecture of all periods from the Moorish Alcazar, Toledo, through Italian and Oxford Renaissance, to the eighteenth century and Regency. Before going to Italy in 1924 the artist had a spell of interior decorating, and previously studied at the Wolverhampton Art School. Primarily a draughtsman with unusual powers of concentration on the intricacies of the domestic or ecclesiastical façade, he is aware that such drawings must be more than façades, and must suggest weight, depth and height. Some of his drawings of English cathedrals are remarkable for their sense of perpendicular perspective. It was Ruskin who called attention to the fact that long perpendicular lines, like horizontal ones, have their vanishing point, and if we stand close to any tall building and look up at it, this illusion must be rendered if we are to achieve an absolutely truthful effect. I mention this to emphasize the care that Causer takes in 'plotting' his drawing, a care that will make him sit for hours, sometimes in a busy crowded street, oblivious to the noise of traffic and the importunings of the casual *amateur d'art,* to whom he half listens with dry humour. Once, when asked by a small boy what the drawing on which he had been engaged all day was worth, he answered, one shilling, a joke that the boy took so seriously as to retreat and return before long with twelve pennies and considerable hope which unfortunately had to be dashed as gently as possible. Causer first exhibited at the Royal Academy in 1923, and has exhibited regularly ever since at the New English and the Royal Institute of Painters in Water-Colours, of which two latter societies he is a member. He is also a member of the Royal Society of Birmingham Artists, has held one-man shows at the Leger Gallery and the Fine Art Society, and is represented in various public galleries.

HASTINGS

WILLIAM SIDNEY CAUSER, R.I.

By permission of the Hastings Museum and Art Gallery.

[15½ × 22½ in.]

CHARLES SYDNEY CHESTON
R.W.S.

b. 1882

IN DAYS when vulgarity of subject and crudity of technique receive much irresponsible praise from fashionable critics and curators of galleries, such a word as 'refinement' would appear to be out of place. But it is a word that I would apply to Cheston's style. His quiet, modest interpretations of street scenes and landscapes have a delicacy of drawing and colour that linger in the mind when ten hundred blatant pictures have been forgotten. In his work as a whole Cheston expresses an eighteenth-century grace of mood, and his water-colours look their best in an environment where all is considered to please the eye and stimulate the sentiment of charm. Neither too detailed nor too sketchy, always in good tone, these drawings are like well-mannered friends whom we are always happy to meet. Cheston studied at the Slade School and is a member of the New English Art Club and the Royal Society of Painters in Water-Colours. It is possible that he was influenced by Wilson Steer, but he is a more comprehensive draughtsman in the water-colour method. Maybe he owes something to the style of Evelyn Cheston, his first wife, for they worked together as artists for many years—years which have been recorded in the biography[1] which was published in 1931. The drawing *Saumur*, reproduced on the opposite page, is typical of Cheston's style with architecture, a middle course between high finish and vague impressionism, with a skilful appreciation of light and shade. Cheston is a constant exhibitor at the societies of which he is a member and at the Royal Academy, and has works in various public collections.

[1] *Life of Evelyn Cheston.* Faber and Faber (1931).

SAUMUR

CHARLES SYDNEY CHESTON, R.W.S.

[9¾ × 14 in.]

189

JOHN HODGKINSON

b. 1883

ORN IN the old classical city of Chester, and showing early an interest in drawing, John Hodgkinson made a study of various arts and crafts, engraving, wood-carving, leatherwork, enamelling and metalwork, and worked for several years in a craftsman's studio in that city. Here he gained practical knowledge of how beautiful things are made, turning to painting in his leisure moments. His knowledge of the Old Masters and their methods was invaluable to him when he was appointed master of the Rugby Art School, from which institution he retired in 1945. A landscape painter of considerable subtlety, Hodgkinson insists on a careful pencil drawing in the first place, holding the view that good drawing is the basis of good painting. Making careful studies of his subject, he works out the picture in his studio, thinking in terms of lines and masses rather than details, simplifying his landscapes in an imaginative way. Thus he can interpret a large downland view with an austerity that emphasizes the structural dignity of the scene. Like some of the early masters, especially his favourite, Cotman, Hodgkinson can find subjects in the most unlikely material—an old gate or fence, a deserted quarry, a derelict warehouse. Such things to him have a mysterious quality that he conveys in restrained colour. The drawing which is reproduced here is more than a few wintry trees and a stretch of tranquil water. It expresses the spirit of the place in its cold, autumnal solitude with a curious ghostly radiance. It is an improvisation on nature, from which all inessential facts have been excluded. Thinking of his picture as a pattern of form and tint, the artist achieves compromise between a decorative and realistic idea of the scene.

THE GHOSTLY WOOD: EARLY AUTUMN

JOHN HODGKINSON

[11 × 15½ in.]

DAME LAURA KNIGHT

D.B.E., R.A., R.W.S.

WHETHER women paint as well as or better than men is the kind of superficial question so irresistible to superficial minds. We look at the history of painting and easily confirm the fact that the overwhelming majority of masters have been men. The creation of great works of art demands a very masculine fortitude and courage, but that is not to say that a few women artists have not been endowed with these virtues; and certainly Dame Laura is conspicuous among the world's women painters, and holds her own place with the best masculine contemporaries. Like all fully creative minds she ranges vastly over vast subjects of exceedingly interesting variety, founding her *œuvre* on the human figure in action or repose. To so powerful a designer of this most intricate structure, all forms of nature are and can be subjects for interpretation. Dame Laura's pictures of the ballet and of the circus command our respect since they could not have been achieved without life-long enthusiasm and indefatigable industry. From the artificial but none the less appealing grace of the Russian ballet to the circus droll and performing horse or elephant the artist moves with that equal assurance born of an intense curiosity. She will turn with no less authority to portraits and landscapes, and I remember with no little pleasure how she once traced the austere if aged splendour of some Richmond Park oak-trees well known to me. Her series of war pictures culminating in the drama of the Nuremberg Trials will be of special interest to the future, for they are historic documents as well as works of art. Like all fine artists Dame Laura has allowed nature to be her supreme teacher, avoiding the theories that have made havoc of much contemporary painting. She has not stuttered in the precious idiom barely comprehended by even those who practise it, but has 'spoken' eloquently to the multitude of normal beings. Hence the deserved popularity of her work. R.A., R.W.S., R.E., and Hon.LL.D. of St Andrew's University, she began her studies at the Nottingham School of Art, won many medals and scholarships, and has works in public galleries all over the world.

MARY AND THE PONIES
DAME LAURA KNIGHT, D.B.E., R.A., R.W.S.

By permission of the Laing Art Gallery, Newcastle-upon-Tyne.
[$18\frac{1}{8} \times 22\frac{1}{4}$ in.]

RANDOLPH SCHWABE
R.W.S.

1885–1948

AT A TIME when nothing is constant but inconstancy, the Slade School may count itself fortunate in professors who have remained steadfast to a certain degree of classicism. Revolutions in art, or in politics for that matter, are alien to the British temperament, and our genius is, or was, inherent in evolution, a far wiser conception of the idea of progress. With Legros, Fred Brown, Wilson Steer, and Schwabe, the Slade has consistently taught its students to draw and to discipline themselves to what the eye can see, and not to follow the will-o'-the-wisp of abstractionism or surrealistics. It is incumbent in an art-master to demonstrate in his own works the solution of problems, and Schwabe's drawings are an example of what can be done with pen and pencil to realize the most intricate architecture. Portrait painting is not confined only to faces. Houses, palaces, churches and streets should be recognizable, especially in an age which does not hesitate to sweep away such masterpieces as Adam's Adelphi Terrace and Nash's Regent Street. Therefore such an artist as Schwabe, in recording what survivals remain, was not only expressing an aesthetic necessity but holding in trust, as it were, for posterity, the features of admirable architectural creations. In the course of time Pelham Crescent, Hastings, a delightful relic, must pass into oblivion, but not, we hope, for many years. This is a very subtle vista of early nineteenth-century bricks and mortar, and knowing it well I venture to say that the artist has drawn it with impeccable skill. In a sense, Schwabe was with the best topographical draughtsmen, Farington, Malton and Boys. He was born in Manchester, studied at the Slade and in Paris, was made Professor of Fine Art at the Slade in 1930, and was a member of the New English Art Club, in addition to being an R.W.S. He was also an authority on costume and collaborated with F. M. Kelly on *Historic Costume, A Chronicle of Fashion in Western Europe,* and *A Short History of Costume and Armour.*

PELHAM CRESCENT, HASTINGS
RANDOLPH SCHWABE, R.W.S.

By permission of the Hastings Museum and Art Gallery.
[11½ × 11½ in.]

ALFRED EGERTON COOPER

R.B.A., A.R.C.A.

b. 1885

IT HAS often been argued whether versatility is a virtue or a handicap, and the only answer is that it depends on time and place. The artists of the Renaissance were most versatile. Sculptor, painter, architect and poet were frequently combined in one personality. *Ve un arta sola,* said Alfred Stevens, a supreme sculptor, painter and architect (1818–75). His idea was that art was a unity, whatever the medium of expression. But times have changed since the *cinquecento*. The world is too clamorous, there are too many people and too many interests. To gain the applause of the crowd and attract attention, the modern artist has to specialize in some particular subject, and in some cases to 'stunt' about like an unlicensed clown. Quite a few modernists have became famous, temporarily albeit, for their own individual kind of opportunism. Egerton Cooper is among the versatile artists. He has spent his life learning how to paint anything and everything, using all methods, oil, tempera, water-colour, gouache, charcoal, and pencil, with great facility. I know of few artists who could render such a diversity of subjects—straight portraits, crowds of figures, nudes, landscapes, buildings, flowers, animals—in so accomplished a style. In Cooper the pictorial sense is very highly developed, and if it is not the business of artists to make pictures I do not know what their function is. Such knowledge, such technical assurance, combined with an unquenchable enthusiasm, make Cooper a good teacher, and quite a few of the younger generation have been helped up the ladder of fame by his practical assistance and encouragement. The artist's experience of the Old Masters' work and their methods is profound, and his vast studio, in Glebe Place, Chelsea, generally contains in addition to his own work interesting examples by the painters of the past. Cooper's water-colours, whether transparent or in bodycolour, come into the category of expert sketching, and to watch him deal expeditiously with a half-imperial size water-colour is a lesson in itself. He exhibits regularly at the Royal Academy and other societies.

NUDE
ALFRED EGERTON COOPER, R.B.A., A.R.C.A.

[$10\frac{1}{2} \times 14\frac{1}{2}$ in.]

197

HENRY RUSHBURY

R.A., R.W.S., R.E.

b. 1889

It was J. M. W. Turner who dubbed David Cox 'Farmer' Cox, probably on account of his healthy, weather-beaten features and deliberate style of life. Henry Rushbury also looks as if he were associated with farms and broad acres, and conversant with the rotation of crops; and it is an interesting fact that Rushbury was born at Harborne, Birmingham, the place to which Cox retired and where he eventually died. But whereas Cox had a tantalizing variety of styles in art, Rushbury has remained consistent to a method that he has made essentially his own. He comes into the category of modern topographical draughtsmen, using a precise pen or pencil line washed in with tints. He has carried on the tradition of artists like Farington and Rooker, and his many records of townscapes at home and abroad will be as interesting to posterity as is the work of the earlier masters. There is a certain elegance about Rushbury's work that enlivens the architectural facts, which he understands and adapts for pictorial effect. For many years the artist's urban scenes have been a feature of the London exhibitions, but he is equally adept, as in the view of *Looe* reproduced on the opposite page, in rendering a pleasant synthesis of land and seascape. There is a certain logic about Rushbury's work that appeals to the classical mind in contradistinction to the pseudo-romanticism now so fashionable but so unsuitable to the architectural subject. The artist was made a member of the Royal Academy in 1936, and of the Royal Society of Painters in Water-Colours in 1927. He is also a member of the Royal Society of Painters, Etchers and Engravers, and of the New English Art Club. His drawings and paintings of London in wartime, now in the Imperial War Museum, have a historic as well as an aesthetic value.

LOOE

HENRY RUSHBURY, R.A., R.W.S., R.E.

[13¼ × 17½ in.]

199

CHARLES CUNDALL

R.A., R.W.S.

b. 1890

To encounter Charles Cundall coming home in the autumn dusk over the Sussex hill, carrying a large canvas, is to be aware of his quiet determination to look into the heart of nature. Painting to such a scale in the open air is a test of physical and nervous power, and it accounts for the fresh and luminous qualities to be seen in the artist's landscape work. Cundall has painted much of late years in Sussex, where he and his wife, Jacqueline, herself an artist of distinction, escape from the busy hum of Chelsea town. Cundall's landscapes are always deservedly prominent at the Royal Academy, the Royal Society of Painters in Water-Colours, and the New English Art Club. He not only excels in landscapes, but his urban scenes, with architectural backgrounds crowded with figures, are also an indication of a versatile grasp of many subjects of pictorial value. Born in 1890, he studied at the Royal College of Art and the Slade School, and in Paris. Of the many artists known to the author of this book, Cundall, it would seem, has contrived to live and to paint much as he wishes, and though fame has come upon him it is due to the merit of his work rather than to any passionate desire for prominence. His love of travelling about the world is no less than his devotion to his work. Time was when one might meet Cundall sketching happily enough on Broadway, New York, and trying at the same time to listen to the comments of a negro who thought himself divinely endowed with the power of filling in lines with colour. Or one might meet the Cundalls in Anticoli, or Rome or Toledo, or some remote village of the Alpes Maritimes, or Galway or Wales or Scotland. None the less, Cundall, by reason of his skill in recording historic events, is able to indulge his *wanderlust* even in these days. A royal tour to be recorded, and the artist will be part of the retinue; a historic battle to complete the records of the second World War, and Cundall will be off to Sicily. But perhaps Cundall is happiest when interpreting some scene remote from actuality, in Sussex, or on the Continent, such as the impressive view of Segovia, Spain, reproduced on the opposite page.

SEGOVIA

Charles Cundall, R.A., R.W.S.

By permission of Geoffrey Cumberlege, Esq.

[14 × 18 in.]

201

LEONARD RUSSELL SQUIRRELL

R.E., R.W.S.

b. 1893

As a draughtsman, particularly, Squirrell is very skilful. He sees nature as an arrangement of lines and masses, and draws his subject out of doors, using the pencil or pen with care and deliberation, writing notes of colour on his drawing. He then reconstructs the scene in his studio. Squirrell prefers the considered composition instead of the rapid snapshot of nature which we have come to associate with impressionism. The artist accentuates contrasts between light and dark objects, interchanging in the same composition. These, with subtle opposing of the general drift of lines, plus a full vision of the whole scene, make for rich comprehensive effect. His style is the result of many panoramic drawings, birds'-eye views of towns, extensive landscapes, trees, ruins, which he delighted in as a student. Though he admits that his favourite master is Cotman, and has undoubtedly derived something from the forerunner's genius for patterning, Squirrell is no furtive manipulator of Cotman's easily plagiarized style. He works in water-colour, oil, pastel and the various forms of etching, but chiefly water-colour, in which he prefers the direct and transparent wash, and not body-colour. Squirrell believes in a fairly restricted palette (eight to ten colours), and sometimes uses a quiet range of colour in combination with a careful sepia pen-line. The artist was born at Ipswich on October 30, 1893, and studied at the Ipswich School of Art and the Slade School. He began etching about 1913, gaining the British Institution Scholarship in Engraving in 1915. At the International Print Makers' Exhibitions at Los Angeles he gained the Silver Medal in 1923, and the Gold Medal in 1925 and 1930. He first exhibited at the Royal Academy in 1912 at the age of nineteen, and has done so ever since. He was elected an associate of the Royal Society of Painter-Etchers in 1917, and Fellow in 1919. He became a member of the Royal Institute of Painters in Water-Colours in 1932, resigning this on his election in 1935 as Associate to the Royal Society of Painters in Water-Colours, of which he became a full member in 1941.

BANKS OF THE TEME, NEAR LUDLOW
LEONARD RUSSELL SQUIRRELL, R.E., R.W.S.

[10 × 14 in.]

203

JOSEPH McCULLOCH

A.R.W.S.

b. 1893

I F MORLAND, Ibbetson and Rowlandson could now frequent a certain happy rendezvous in Chelsea, I fancy they would find Joe McCulloch a convivial personality after their own hearts, for Joe has the gift of taking most things, except his art, with a laughing philosophy. 'Time is made for slaves,' as Alfred Gilbert once reminded me in Rome, when we sat drinking wine until the small hours; and I do not doubt that this truism has occurred to McCulloch, for he never seems to notice that it is past midnight, though that does not prevent him from an early breakfast and concentration on the day's work. He is a Yorkshireman, with a great love for the country round Leeds where he was born. A Royal Exhibitor in Painting to the Royal College of Art at the age of eighteen, McCulloch has developed a strong personal style in landscape and figure work, a knowledge that he endeavours to impart to students at the Goldsmith's College where he is painting instructor. The artist has a fruitful versatility of subject, and can handle the Yorkshire landscape with a certain instinctive sense of its particular character, not excluding such incidentals as cattle which are, in themselves, always a test of drawing skill. Of late years McCulloch has developed a style of interpreting the architecture of London streets and squares, and has recorded many of those sedate early-Victorian houses in the Chelsea area which have, in the whirligig of time and social discord, assumed a palatial dignity as compared with prefabricated structures of a more enlightened age. McCulloch also understands the intricate structure of ships, and some of his drawings of sailing boats and merchantmen are realized with a fundamental solidity—for instance the ship at the *Victoria Docks* reproduced on the opposite page. He is also an illustrator, and among his work in this direction are the drawings to S. P. B. Mais's *Highways and Byways in the Welsh Marches,* 1939. McCulloch was made an Associate of the Royal Society of Painters in Water-Colours in 1944.

VICTORIA DOCKS, LONDON

JOSEPH McCULLOCH, A.R.W.S.

[11 × 14½ in.]

205

ERNEST MICHAEL DINKEL

A.R.W.S.

b. 1894

PRIMARILY interested in the form of things, Dinkel has the gift of making familiar objects appear 'rich and strange'. This is important, for it adds a creative value to visual facts. How easy it is to pass by a collection of derelict cart wheels or any discarded lumber without seeing that even these can be beautiful and mysterious in shape and colour. The artist can give them a fascinating appearance, without resort to eccentric drawing or improbable colour, by his own penetrating and truthful vision. It is Dinkel's very insistence on form and patterning that makes us stop and look at such drawings. His own intense curiosity stimulates ours. His method of tinting is direct and lucid on a carefully arranged design. Dinkel was born at Huddersfield in 1894, studied at the Technical College and School of Art there, and later at the Royal College of Art, where he was also a teacher. He won the Owen Jones Travelling Scholarship in 1926. From 1940 to 1948 he was Principal of the Stourbridge School of Arts and Crafts, and is now Head of the School of Design at the Edinburgh College of Art. Dinkel also works in stained glass and designs table glass and murals. He is represented in the Tate Gallery; the Laing Art Gallery, Newcastle-upon-Tyne; and the Dudley Art Gallery.

AGRICULTURAL MEDLEY
Ernest Michael Dinkel, A.R.W.S.

[11 × 13½ in.]

AVERIL BURLEIGH

A.R.W.S.

d. 1949

THOUGH she lived all her life in Brighton and the neighbourhood, Averil Burleigh, until the late war, painted much abroad and after that found Wales an inspiring centre. She married C. H. Burleigh, R.O.I., 'under whose influence, principally, she developed her artistic expression, first in tempera and later in water-colour landscape and oil figure subjects'. Mrs Burleigh combined a realistic and decorative vision. She searched for design in nature; and her tree drawing shows considerable knowledge and feeling for the subject. The water-colour reproduced on the opposite page was painted in the neighbourhood of Bettws-y-Coed, and is a typical example of her sensitive method of suggesting foliage and other form by the use of a semi-dry brush dragged lightly over the surface of the paper. Her effects were gained by lucid washes of colour over a careful pencil or chalk drawing. Mrs Burleigh is represented in several public galleries, including Leeds, Belfast, Brighton, Hove and Worthing.

THE WOODCUTTERS
AVERIL BURLEIGH, A.R.W.S.

[10 × 14 in.]

CHARLES KNIGHT
R.W.S., R.O.I.

b. 1901

FROM his house at Ditchling, Charles Knight has access to some of the best painting country in England. Not far away is Lewes and the Downs, and many little villages with old manor houses and parish churches that appear to nestle discreetly under the wings of Time. Having been born in Brighton in 1901, Knight learned in boyhood the highways and byways of his native Sussex. If artists as a general rule are born peripatetics, they are inclined to do their best work in an environment that they understand. Hence many landscape-painters are identified with certain tracts of country that are familiar to them, however they may for the sake of change explore pastures new. Constable, Crome and Cotman are as much part of East Anglia as the very subjects they painted with such distinction. T. M. Richardson is associated with the country round Newcastle-upon-Tyne; Collier must have learned the alphabet, at least, of his art in the moorland scenery of the Derbyshire Peak; Turner (of Oxford) is remembered in many a Cotswold view. There are, of course, exceptional geniuses, like J. M. W. Turner, who could take all nature for their province and excel in whatever they touched. Charles Knight is a traditionalist, and has been influenced by Cotman in a sense of design and patterning, but retains his own personal attitude and fine colour. Technically he is among the most accomplished of contemporary water-colourists, and it is always a delight to follow the confidence of his brush work. He studied at the Brighton School of Art and the Royal Academy Schools, and won the Turner Gold Medal, He is represented in the Tate Gallery, the British Museum, and in collections at Newcastle, Leeds, Hull and elsewhere.

THE FALLEN TREE
CHARLES KNIGHT, R.W.S., R.O.I.

[10¼ × 14¾ in.]

CHARLES F. TUNNICLIFFE

A.R.A., R.E.

b. 1901

IN HIS autobiography called *My Country Book*, discussing his student days at the Royal College of Art, Tunnicliffe makes these significant remarks: 'And while those students who talked much rolled out the names of Cézanne, Gauguin and Matisse, I was more interested in the work of certain other masters—Piero della Francesca, Pieter Breughel, Hans Memlinc, Albrecht Dürer, and, nearer to our own time, John Constable, Thomas Girtin, and John Sell Cotman. We all had our gods.' 'Gods' is the word. Tunnicliffe had no difficulty in his choice, and the result is that he has won an unequivocal place in contemporary painting. Son of a farmer, he combines a practical knowledge of the land with the artist's love for all the seasonable form and colour of nature. He has the advantage over the urban-born artist in that the subjects for his pencil and brush are his familiars, part of his country experience. Painter and wood-engraver, he shows a comprehensive delight in all rural things from a blade of grass to a bull, from an old weather-beaten fence to a flock of birds on the wing. The best of all gifts, perhaps, is a combination of the naturalist's eye, the heart of the poet, and the hand of the craftsman. With such one has the key to the treasures of nature, and all artists of any distinction possess to a lesser or greater extent this gift. It is certainly a part of Tunnicliffe's temperament. Thus endowed, an artist may well realize his dream of communicating not with one generation only but with posterity, and though the scientific and totalitarian trend of events would appear to militate against individual achievement, and the immediate future of art for this reason was never so obscure, we can be certain, at least, that there will always be men and women who will derive happiness in the contemplation of nature and the art that nature inspires.

GREBE FIRST-BORN

CHARLES F. TUNNICLIFFE, A.R.A., R.E.

[14 × 21½ in.]

CLAUDE MUNCASTER

R.W.S., R.O.I., S.M.A.

b. 1903

THE KEY to Claude Muncaster's art and temperament may be found in the fact that he once sailed before the mast from Australia round Cape Horn in a four-masted barque. For a young man, in these days, such an experience is almost unique. In fact, there can be very few sailors left even of the older generation who can claim such an adventure. Muncaster has described it in his book *Rolling Round the Horn*. It used to be thought that artists were somewhat timid and unadventurous souls; and this idea was probably due to the 'ivory tower' attitude of the pre-Raphaelite mood, and the 'preciosities' of the 'nineties. We have only to recall such lives as those of William Havell, John Glover, David Roberts, and other water-colourists to realize that Muncaster is in the true tradition of artist-adventurers. His bold style in the water-colour method expresses a robust point of view, and he handles a variety of subjects including landscapes, shipping (he is a member of the Society of Marine Artists), and buildings with equal skill. Muncaster is particularly good at mountain scenes, with great skies, in which the effect of sunlight and shadow is rendered with a direct, convincing touch. So lucid and candid is his style that it is a lesson as to how a water-colour should be painted—that direct, straightforward statement which, of course, is the result of constant practice. The artist is among the youngest exhibitors at the Royal Academy, for he was only seventeen when his first exhibit appeared on the walls of Burlington House. He held his first one-man show at the Fine Arts Society when he was twenty-three, and was elected to the Royal Society of Painters in Water-Colours in 1931. During his various voyages round the world he has acquired a sailor's knowledge of ships, and draws sailing craft with commendable accuracy. In 1947 he was granted the privilege of staying with Their Majesties at Balmoral in order to complete a series of pictures the Queen had commissioned him to paint of Windsor, Sandringham and Balmoral. This privilege was remarkable in that whilst certain portrait painters have lived and worked at Court, the number of landscape-painters who have enjoyed a similar privilege must be extraordinarily small.

WHARFSIDE, GREENWICH
CLAUDE MUNCASTER, R.W.S., R.O.I., S.M.A.

By permission of G. E. Garland, Esq.
[9 × 14 in.]

215

THOMAS HENNELL

R.W.S.

1903–44

MYSTIC, poet, artist and man of action, Thomas Hennell is among the most remarkable personalities in this breviary of water-colourists. Of the many interesting lives recorded in this book, Hennell's, perhaps, combines the greatest contrasts in peace and strife. His romantic imagination and transcendental intuitions could not have visualized a more adventurous passage through life than happened to him. Hennell had a gentle, child-like temperament, not unlike Blake's, with a religious fervour for every manifestation of beauty. His friend, Vincent Lines, informs me that to walk with Hennell in the country was a memorable experience. To hear him talk about the simplest, ordinary details of nature, even a stone in the road, was to listen to an inspired utterance. Hennell was a true countryman, and with the artist's curiosity in all things of rustic significance, and he made the most fastidious drawings of farm wagons and agricultural implements for books on country crafts. These things were loved by Hennell as much for their beauty and utility as for their symbolical meaning in the eternal pageant of life. When the second World War came, he was engaged in making water-colours for the 'Recording Britain' scheme, and then devoted his talents to recording the war on various fronts. He developed from his precise draughtsmanship into a style appropriate to the speed and action of modern warfare—a brief, emotional calligraphy that seized on the essentials of the moment. He was for a time in Iceland, then accompanied the troops to France, and finally to the Far East whence he did not return. He was killed in Indonesia. The exact particulars of Hennell's death remain unknown. With a group of other Englishmen he was besieged in a hotel in Surabaya in Java during the uprising. The others got away, but Hennell was last seen surrounded by an excited mob in the courtyard of the hotel. It was reported that he was taken prisoner. No further information was received and nearly a year later the Air Ministry officially recorded his death. Hennell was the author of *Change in the Farm, Poems, The Witness, British Craftsmen, The Countryman at Work.*

MOULIN DESHODT, WORMHOUDT, NORD, FRANCE

THOMAS HENNELL, R.W.S.

By permission of Rex Wailes, Esq.
[20 × 19 in.]

ERIC RAVILIOUS

1908 –42

WHILE on duty as an official war artist Ravilious lost his life in an R.A.F. flight from Iceland, and thus the world was deprived of a water-colourist with a distinct personality. His experience as wood-engraver, book-illustrator, and designer of pottery and glass gave his work an unusual feeling for structure. Ravilious had a style which might be described as 'metallic'. The wash is restricted within a rigid formula—a kind of mosaic of tint—and the whole drawing is built up of pieces, giving it a kaleidoscopic intensity. Within the limits of this method the artist achieved some interesting results. Particularly effective are those drawings done while on duty in northern latitudes. Some of his seascapes scintillate with a diamond-like effect, and would appear to be very true to the cold and barren atmosphere of the far northern land and seascape. How he would have developed from this style is a matter of speculation, but his work does show that Ravilious could improvise in a sincere and useful manner. He had unusual powers of concentration, and could make the most commonplace subjects interesting simply by reason of the fact that he himself was intensely interested in them, not only for the pictorial result, but for their textural quality. Here his knowledge of pottery and glass work was of value to him as a draughtsman. Ravilious was born in London, and studied at the Eastbourne School of Art and at the Royal College of Art where he later became an instructor in drawing.

NORWAY, 1940
ERIC RAVILIOUS

By permission of the Laing Art Gallery, Newcastle-upon-Tyne.

[$17\frac{5}{8} \times 22\frac{5}{8}$ in.]

STUART MILNER
R.B.A., A.R.W.S.

b. 1909

How best to train to become an artist is always a problem. Schools cannot make artists, but can only foster talent and indicate how best to use it. Milner writes that he had no art-school training worthy of mention, but at the age of sixteen and a half went into the studio of Messrs Maple & Co., as a designer of interior decoration and furniture. During his spare time he studied painting from nature. I quote from his letter to me, expressing his attitude towards his art. 'I spent every available moment of spare time painting from nature, my sketching grounds being the City, the riverside at Hammersmith, Chiswick and Kew, Chiswick Park, Hampton Court; and in 1936 I "discovered" the Yorkshire Dales. I have painted in many counties, but after Yorkshire they all seem rather tame. I confess that I have a one-track mind about Yorkshire and its people, and proclaim with childish delight my Yorkshire ancestry, and kinship to two branches of the family still living in the county. The grandeur of the fells, the magnificent rivers and dales, castles and abbeys, the superb timber, the hidden rocky becks, and, pervading all, the rich colour and wonderful variety of climate—they make Yorkshire the perfect painting country. No wonder Cotman, Turner, Girtin and de Wint painted such masterpieces there.' None the less, Milner is an expert sketcher of simple themes with buildings such as the one of *The Lighthouse, Shoreham*, reproduced opposite. He first exhibited at the Royal Academy in 1933, and was elected a member of the Royal Society of British Artists in 1936 and an Associate of the Royal Society of Painters in Water-Colours in 1947, both on the first occasion of application. Recently he has given much time to oil-painting, concentrating on still-life, portraiture and landscape. He admits to having been much influenced by A. W. Rich.

THE LIGHTHOUSE, SHOREHAM
STUART MILNER, R.B.A., A.R.W.S.

[$11\frac{3}{8} \times 13\frac{7}{8}$ in.]

221

VINCENT LINES

R.W.S.

b. 1910

As a student at the Central School of Arts and Crafts under A. S. Hartrick, Vincent Lines was certain of a firm foundation in draughtsmanship. Later, at the Royal College of Art he won the Drawing Prize and Travelling Scholarship, and became the Principal of the Horsham School of Art. Now Principal of the Hastings School of Art, Lines is continuously busy in instructing the younger generation and in his own creative work. Though steeped in tradition he is none the less aware that every artist who wishes to leave something of interest to posterity, must offer his own quota of knowledge and experience to what has been done before. His sensitive drawing derives no doubt from Hartrick's expressive touch, but Lines has added his own skill and imagination, and his water-colours have an essential lyrical feeling which is part of the artist's reaction to life itself. The poet in him responds to the subtler manifestations of the spirit to be seen in the works of William Blake, Samuel Palmer and Lines's friend the late Thomas Hennell, rather than to the realists of water-colour painting; but he is not prejudiced about any style provided it is sincere in the pursuit of truth. Like some of the earlier water-colourists Lines has been fortunate in various commissions, for instance the making of a series of drawings of Windsor and the Park, Bramshill in Hampshire, and other places of beauty. For many years he has been in the habit of cycling or walking about England, Wales and Ireland in search of places to sketch, but being domiciled in Hastings, at the top of a tall house overlooking the sea, Lines has added many drawings of the characteristic old town to the work of the forerunners—Prout, Havell, Cox and Badham—who also found Hastings full of subjects of pictorial interest. *The Long Walk, Windsor,* reproduced on the opposite page, is an important record, since the elm trees, planted by Charles II, no longer exist. Suffering from blight, they had to be felled in 1943.

THE LONG WALK, WINDSOR

VINCENT LINES, R.W.S.

By gracious permission of H.M. the King.

[15 × 22 in.]

ALBERT RICHARDS

1919–45

ALBERT RICHARDS is among the youngest artists in this anthology. He was born in Liverpool, and studied at the Central School, Wallasey, from which he passed by scholarship to the Wallasey School of Arts and Crafts. In September 1940 he was awarded a Wallasey Major Scholarship, tenable at the Royal College of Arts, London. He joined the Royal Engineers before his first year at the College was completed, and continued to paint pictures in his leisure time. Richards was determined to become an Official War Artist, and persisted against every pessimistic opinion. The War Office offered him a short-time commission in 1942. This he would not accept until finally they made him an Official War Artist in the General Services Branch. Richards dropped with the Sixth Airborne Division on D-Day, 'and laying aside his sketch book in order to command his unit in the Caen area was killed by a mine near the River Maas. . . .' He was about to paint a night attack over the Maas. Richards was an artist of exceptional power, and a student of old and new styles of water-colour work, always insisting on strong drawing, and interpreting form and colour with an imaginative touch. His war pictures, particularly those in which aeroplanes and gliders appear, are instinct with forceful realism and large design. The stark beauty and significance of these accessories of modern war, reacting on a sensitive mind, produced many vivid war records. Although so young, he had achieved sufficient fine work to promise a great career, and it is regretted that fate intervened before he could completely fulfil himself as an artist.

GLIDER CRASH-LANDED AGAINST BRIDGE

ALBERT RICHARDS

By permission of the Walker Art Gallery, Liverpool.

[21 × 29 in.]

BIBLIOGRAPHY

History of the 'Old Water-Colour' Society, by J. L. Roget.

The Old Water-Colour Society's Club Volumes, 1923–48, with special reference to the work therein of Randall Davies, F.S.A., Martin Hardie, Hon. R.W.S., C.B.E., Hesketh Hubbard, V.-P. R.B.A., F.S.A., and Iolo A. Williams.

The Catalogue of Pictures and Drawings in the Collection of Frederick John Nettlefold, Esq., by C. Reginald Grundy and F. Gordon Roe, F.S.A.

The Farington Diary, edited by James Greig.

Chronological History of the Old English Landscape Painters, by Colonel M. H. Grant.

History of Water-Colour Painting in England, by Gilbert Redgrave.

The English Water-Colour Painters, by C. E. Hughes.

British Water-Colour Art, by Marcus Huish.

History of British Water-Colour Painting, by H. M. Cundall, I.S.O.

Landscape in English Art and Poetry, by Laurence Binyon.

Thomas Girtin and English Water-Colours, by Laurence Binyon.

English Water-Colours, by Laurence Binyon.

Thomas Girtin's Water-Colours, by Randall Davies, F.S.A.

Water-Colour Painting, by Alfred William Rich.

John Sell Cotman, by Sydney D. Kitson.

Artists and Their Friends in England, 1700–99, by W. T. Whitley.

Memoirs of the Life of John Constable, by C. R. Leslie, edited by the Hon. Andrew Shirley.

Life of Samuel Palmer, by A. H. Palmer.

Hercules Brabazon Brabazon, by C. Lewis Hind.

W. J. Wainwright, by Walter Turner.

Cox the Master, by F. Gordon Roe, F.S.A.

Thomas Rowlandson, by F. Gordon Roe, F.S.A.

Thomas Collier, R.I., by Adrian Bury.

John Varley of the 'Old Society', by Adrian Bury.

Water-Colour Painting of Today (Studio Special Number), by Adrian Bury.

Sandby Drawings at Windsor, by Paul Oppé, C.H.

Alexander Cozens; Illustrated Catalogue of Tate Gallery Exhibition 1946 (December), by Paul Oppé, C.H.

Life of J. M. W. Turner, by A. J. Finberg.

BIBLIOGRAPHY

Modern Painters, by John Ruskin.

A Century of British Painters, by Samuel and Richard Redgrave.

Memoir of Peter de Wint and William Hilton, by Harriet de Wint.

Memorials of F. O. Finch, by Mrs. Finch.

Catalogue of Water-Colour Paintings (1927), Victoria and Albert Museum.

Volumes of the Walpole Society.

Illustrated Catalogue of the Permanent Collection of Water-Colours in the Laing Art Gallery, Newcastle-upon-Tyne, by C. Bernard Stevenson.

Augustus Walker's Quarterlies on the Old English Water-Colour Painters.

The Connoisseur.

The Studio, (including all the Special Numbers on Water-Colour Painters).

Bryan's Dictionary of Painters and Engravers.

Dictionary of National Biography.

227

1350 S
Buck